AIRPLAY

AIRPLAY

An Anthology of CBC Radio Drama

Airplay: An Anthology of CBC Radio Drama
first published 1996 by
Scirocco Drama
An imprint of J. Gordon Shillingford Publishing Inc.
© 1996

Cover design by Terry Gallagher/Doowah Design

Printed and bound in Canada by Les Ateliers Graphiques Marc Veilleux

Published with the generous assistance of The Canada Council

Canadian Cataloguing in Publication Data

Main entry under title:
    Airplay: an anthology of CBC radio drama

ISBN 1-896239-11-0

    1. Radio plays, Canadian (English) I. Carley,
Dave, 1955-

PS8309.R34A38 1996   C812'.022080054   C96-900902-X
PR9196.7.R34A38 1996

For Carl and Darina

ACKNOWLEDGEMENTS

First and foremost, I would like to cite (and applaud) the achievements of Damiano Pietropaolo, Area Head of Radio Performance, and James Roy, Executive Producer of *Sunday Showcase*, who together have revived and energized radio drama in this country, even as the budgetary sun sets. Also, my gratitude goes out to the five talented Producers of the dramas in this volume: David Britton, Martie Fishman, Lynda Hill, James Roy and Gregory J. Sinclair. And, of course, sitting beside every talented Producer there is an equally talented Associate Producer: Sandra Jeffries-Broitman, Nina Callaghan and Kate Nickerson. Prior to the studio there is the effervescent Casting Director Linda Grearson and, in the studio, there are the amazing actors who bring these dramas to life. Thanks also to my fellow Script Editors at Radio Performance, Emil Sher and Shelley Tepperman.

Above all, my gratitude and enduring respect are owed to the playwrights with whom I work at Radio Performance and, especially, to Lorre Jensen, Emil Sher, Judith Thompson, George F. Walker and Rachel Wyatt.

TABLE OF CONTENTS

AirPlay's editor, Dave Carley, is an award-winning playwright whose plays have been produced across Canada and the United States, as well as in England, Australia, New Zealand and Japan. His works include *Writing With Our Feet*, *Taking Liberties*, *Into*, *After You* and *A View from the Roof*. Dave has also written extensively for radio, and is the senior script editor for CBC Radio Performance.

INTRODUCTION

I WAS ONCE ASKED TO SIT on a panel of dramaturges. It was to be a blue chip group of theatre thinkers and I was expected to pontificate on my theories of dramaturgy. I suppose I should have been flattered but instead I was terrified. Luckily I had a prior engagement—a root canal operation or something. I was saved from that horrifying moment when I'd have to admit in front of a live audience that I actually have no theories. Or, more particularly, that I have a multitude of theories but none of them pertinent to the art of dramaturgy. Or, to be absolutely exact, if I did have a theory of dramaturgy it was essentially an anti-theory.

I am the script editor for *Sunday Showcase* and *Monday Night Playhouse*, the two hour-long drama series on the Canadian Broadcasting Corporation's AM and FM bands. Before that I was the editor of *Stereodrama*—another hour-long series—and prior to that, the editor for the dramas that aired on *Morningside*. (I've always preferred "script editor" to "dramaturge", which feels like a somewhat exalted and pretentious description of what I do.) In the eight years I've been in the Mother Corporation's Radio Performance department I should have had plenty of time to form a few dramaturgical doctrines to amaze and delight panel-goers. But before I was a script editor I was (and still am) a playwright, and I think this is the real genesis of my anti-theory of dramaturgy.

The playwright, as victim. We all have stories. I remember sitting in a rehearsal hall once with a director-slash-dramaturge and a few actors, feeling exceedingly naked. The director was demanding that I describe "the journey" of my central character (the travel agent school of dramaturgy). I remember answering that the essence of my central character was his utter journeylessness; that what he was on the first page he remained on the last, to the great detriment of everyone and everything in between. This was not viewed as a satisfactory response; it was somehow anti-dramatic and also, as I recall, anti-life affirming (the pro-life school of dramaturgy). But I was young then and naively allowed myself to be turned. I set about creating an arc for my arcless character, and ruined my play.

I have since come to know and love many playwrights and, over coffee and better, we invariably trade similar stories. Everyone has had a prescription for us. Everyone has a theory that will save our scripts, if only we will bend over and submit. We, of course, just want to write. Now, I don't mean to slag dramaturges, and I should pause here for a little definitional charity. In this country the dramaturgical role is usually filled by the director, with actors occasionally self-anointing themselves, along with anyone else who can pronounce the word. Only a couple of theatres have the luxury of a resident, European-style dramaturge who is able to embrace the continuum of play development. The best dramaturges—generally those rare, full-time ones—are so good, so enthusiastic and so supportive they actually make you want to write. The worst ones— usually the self-anointed—come densely packed with theory. Theories, I've learned, are the suburbs of agendas. And those agendas are legion, overt and covert, political and stylistic: feminist, left or further left or neo-con, structuralist or post-structuralist, pro-internals, pro-streams of consciousness, anti-narrator, anti-narrative, anti-sex... The list goes on and meanwhile the stupid dramaturges are swarming all over our scripts like children in a grade school pile-on.

So now that someone's actually paying me to poke around other writers' radio dramas, I'm understandably a bit theory-shy. I refuse to believe there's a right or wrong way to create a radio play that can exist independently of and prior to the birth of that script.

As script editor at CBC Radio Performance's department—a part-time position—I work on about twenty-five plays a year. The amount of time spent on each script varies radically—some writer-editor relationships are fleeting and others are astonishingly intimate. On average, I probably read each of the three drafts we contractually require five times—and there are often more "volunteer" drafts. Each draft is followed by extended meetings with the writers. I also do a fair bit of collateral research, as I have discovered that even our noblest writers will play fast and loose with facts— which is fine if it suits some dramatic purpose but, when unintentional, only serves to fire up our legions of sharp-eared listeners. Ultimately the workload means that many scripts do the Topsy thing—they just grow on their own, in inadvertent support of my own theories of non-prescription.

The radio plays in this volume are radically different in tone and style and required different editorial tacks. Rachel Wyatt's dramatization of a novel (*Crackpot*) invited a very different response from that required by what is essentially a stage play for radio (George F.

Walker's *How to Make Love to an Actor*). And the radiophonic imagination of Judith Thompson in *Stop Talking Like That* is light years apart from Emil Sher's docu-dramatic approach in *Mourning Dove*. The gentle, non-interventionist community of Lorre Jensen's *The Mercy Quilt* is a far cry from the staccato conflict of Walker's piece. The authors also ranged from brand new to radio (Lorre Jensen) to one of Canada's most experienced radio dramatists (Rachel Wyatt) and the level of authorial familiarity with the medium must be taken into account by the editor. The broadcast venue is also important. The AM network requirements of *Morningside* (which commissioned and first broadcast *Mourning Dove*) are very different from the stereo network series which commissioned the other four dramas.

IF JANE AUSTEN HAD BEEN MOHAWK, and if she'd grown up on the Tyendinega Mohawk Territory east of Belleville, Ontario, I think she would have written something like *The Mercy Quilt*. Lorre Jensen's play is a portrait of a community bound tightly by social convention, heritage, custom and manners. It's an auspicious radio debut for Jensen, for whom playwriting is a recently acquired addiction. After a twenty-year career in advertising and television production, Jensen wrote *Coming Round,* (with Paula Wing), which was produced at Theatre New Brunswick in 1991. I met her at Cahoots Theatre Projects where she was developing an exhilarating new take on *The Wizard of Oz, The Shaman of Waz*. Her Cahoots play did not reach production, but there was no mistaking Jensen's talent, and when she described *The Mercy Quilt* to the Executive Producer of *Sunday Showcase*, James Roy, he was quick to offer a commission.

The Mercy Quilt recreates the world of Tyendinega, a small reserve in southeastern Ontario. In particular, Jensen takes us into that part of the community inhabited by the Elders, a group of women who have decided to hold a raffle to pay for display cases for a new museum. One of their number has grown increasingly forgetful and, when entrusted with the care of the raffle prize, a beaded necklace with a turtle centrepiece, she promptly gives it away. The others must somehow endeavour to retrieve the necklace (they've already sold hundreds of tickets) without embarrassing their friend. And into the mix arrives Lorraine, who has spent most of her adult life in Toronto, and who no longer understands her elders' desire for non-intervention. What follows is a gentle comedy of manners, as the women seek to both indirectly orchestrate the return of the necklace, and hunt up a suitable suitor for the single Lorraine.

Enter the script editor, who prior to Jensen's script actually had one residual theory of drama that he'd picked up somewhere and harboured like an intellectual tapeworm. "Drama arises from conflict." But *The Mercy Quilt* is all about non-conflict and, particularly, the concept of non-interference. The play is built entirely on the premise that its central characters will go to any lengths—including minor larceny—to avoid conflict with one of their number which might result in embarrassment or humiliation. The city-thinking Lorraine expresses impatience with the subterfuge and suggests they go directly to the forgetful woman's daughter and explain the situation.

LORRAINE: You know, it'd be a lot easier to go to May and explain what's happened.

SARAH: *(Sudden sharp intake of breath.)* Ah.

GRACE: We can't interfere like that, Lorraine.

LORRAINE: But, Ma, it's the truth.

GRACE: Well…sometimes it's kinder to hold back the truth.

And with that Lorraine capitulates. Non-intervention wins the day. "Drama arises from conflict." Now that's a dramaturgical mantra for you. Except that *The Mercy Quilt*—with virtually no conflict of any kind—works admirably. And I can think of no clearer example of the need for a dramaturge or script editor to submit to the demands of the script than here. Jensen's play is rooted in a specific cultural assumption that must be allowed to supersede dramaturgical mantras. If I rebel against the prescription of "journey" for a character, then I must also find a way to accept a play devoid of conflict.

Looking back on my editor's notes, I realize how much I learned during the course of working on this play. The first lesson was to trust that Jensen's ability to create humour and a sense of community would carry the play. The second was to recognize what lies beneath the apparently calm waters of this reserve. My notes from the pre-first draft wondered what were "the stakes" (mantra #2). We seemed to have an entire play predicated on the return of a simple necklace; would this be enough to hold listeners for an hour?

The Mercy Quilt conceals much beneath its gentle folds. The stakes are not the necklace; it is only the objectification of a much larger thing; the battle over cultural precepts. *The Mercy Quilt* is a dramatic exposition of cultural attitudes that are in danger of being lost forever. Tradition, community—it nearly slipped away, the Tyendinega reserve being particularly vulnerable by virtue of its location in Southern Ontario and the length of time it has been in contact with white majoritarian culture. But now, led by the elders, there is a quickening appreciation of what has nearly been lost. In one scene Sarah describes a vision, and Jensen slips out her own thesis, tidily contrasting the spiritual and material world of television (or "teevee" as Marge insists on stressing) in the process.

SARAH: Wanda Shewanda had a vision when she was making the beads.

GRACE: Was she seeing things?

LORRAINE: Go on, Sarah.

SARAH: Happened last spring, after a late snow fall. The water was swollen from the runoff. It was a nice day, she said, and it felt good to be outdoors. She looked down and saw a turtle just stopped by the stoop, like. She asked it where it had come from and went on to say, to commiserate, like, about the long winter just passed. Then it left and went into the water. Soon as it got in, the water turned real blue, just like the beads. She said the water looked just like one of them prizes on *The Price is Right*.

GRACE: Do you believe that?

LORRAINE: Don't you, Ma?

GRACE: Maybe I forgot how to believe. It must be fifty years since anyone on this reserve heard tell of a vision. If you owned up to one today, they'd lock you away. I blame it on them missionaries. We lost a lot on account of them.

MARGE: You don't lose anything unless you agree to let it go.

The Mercy Quilt is Jensen's first radio drama, and that in itself poses a set of challenges for the script editor. Not only was her whole approach to this drama a new one, but there were all the particulars of radio's needs to be mentioned and/or discarded. In some seasons up to half of our dramas are written by writers new to the medium, and this requires an individualized approach of both editing and instruction. The sensitivity to the new writer's needs are heightened by the fact that the balance of experience is so skewed; one must be avoid the temptation to become prescriptive simply by virtue of a longer-standing acquaintanceship with the medium.

Radiophonically, my principal worry with *The Mercy Quilt* was the number of elderly female voices. Radio does many things well, and one of those is its ability to confuse. We hear with our eyes and, when robbed of sight, the presence of four or five elderly voices can become impossible to differentiate. Jensen killed one quilter, in the name of clarity, and she helped identify the rest by continually embedding names in the dialogue, an old radio trick. In real life if someone threads your name into every line of dialogue you can be pretty sure he's trying to sell you something. Radio has different requirements. Despite this, there are still moments when the listener cannot be a hundred percent sure who is speaking, but in *The Mercy Quilt* this may not matter. The play is as much about community as individuals and the quilters pretty much think collectively.

In a play about community, Jensen moved her scenes throughout the reserve and off, from the community centre, bowling alley and Pow-wow, to the various homes of the quilters, the IGA, Legion and the shores of the Bay of Quinte. Each venue required a different aural base. But added to the naturalistic sounds of locale were signature sounds that evoke Jensen's belief that the spiritual is ever present in this community. Throughout the drama there is the rattle of the beads, the recurring "Handsome theme", and the suggestion of the turtle roiling the waters of the Bay. The magic is present and all the stronger for co-existing amidst the bowling alley naturalism of the play.

The Mercy Quilt ends with the turtle centrepiece of the missing necklace being set free in the Bay of Quinte and, in the space of a few seconds, Jensen sums up her play, in both dialogue and sound.

> *(SOUND: Muted turtle rattle fades, water lapping faintly. Footsteps on stones.)*

MAY: Jesus! Look at the water!

LORRAINE: Ooooh!

MARGE: It's a vision.

GRACE: After all these years.

LORRAINE: I wonder what Handsome would make of that.

> *(Music: Flute plays "Handsome" signature. Sound: Fade up of water lapping against shoreline. Fade up the song from the Pow-wow singers.)*

LIKE MOST CANADIAN PLAYWRIGHTS, Emil Sher is non-genre specific. He has written for theatre and film and is a frequent essayist with the *Globe and Mail*. But it is in radio that Sher seems to have most strongly found his niche. Radio, and *Morningside* in particular, has a great appetite for his dramas, which pull heavily from current events and combines Sher's passion for human rights issues with his journalistic background.

Mourning Dove was commissioned by *Morningside*. It was a natural fit, a strongly documentary look at events which had been discussed at length on the program. Sher's play was divided into two half-hour segments—reflecting the more fragmented nature of morning listening—and would be followed by a panel discussion.

One of the great unexplained clichés of radio—and there are many—is that morning and AM network listeners listen to the radio while doing dishes or driving, "background listening". Given the immense size of *Morningside*'s audience, that's an awful lot of dishes and driving. Conversely, the typical audience member for the FM network's *Monday Night Playhouse* is widely believed to lounge in his Lazyboy chair, a tumbler of scotch in hand, immobile until the show's closing credits. It is, however, true that the sound quality of the AM band is not as good and does not allow for as elaborate production values, and it does favour voice. And *Morningside*, as the country's premier current affairs show, has a need for issue-based drama.

Mourning Dove was inspired by the Robert Latimer case in Saskatchewan. Latimer was convicted of murdering his daughter, who was suffering horribly from cerebral palsy, and he was sentenced to ten years in jail. A massive outcry followed his conviction, setting off a series of debates on sentencing and mercy killing. In Sher's drama, the names and jurisdiction were changed but many of the key elements remain—a father, haunted by the physical pain endured by his daughter, who ultimately chooses to kill her through carbon monoxide poisoning. The CBC legal department suggested that calendar descriptions of the Sher drama carefully avoid drawing any direct links to the Latimer case, particularly because at the time of airing, January 1996, it was still under appeal. The legal beagles worried that airing a dramatization which ended with a

guilty verdict for the Latimeresque central character would somehow be in contempt of court.

As always, the lawyers seem to have difficulty drawing a
distinction between fiction and real life events—which actually
points up another merit of a work like *Mourning Dove*. Sher's drama
possesses a power that news clips of the Latimer case can never
convey, because it goes beyond the headlines and takes the listener
into the psyches of the principal players. Lacking any kind of visual
physical reference point, the listener must compensate by creating
his own images. Our imagined picture of Tina, for example, which
we must draw from her breathing and gasps and giggles, is bound
to be stronger than any photograph because we have invested so
much energy in her creation. We become proprietary. Likewise the
closeness of the voices to us, with no visual remove, adds an
intensity. The word "intimate" is forever bandied about in descriptions of radio drama; it's another cliché and, in any event, "imme-
diacy" might be a more accurate word. The voice to ear travel of
radio drama is unimpeded. As a result, response to Sher's drama
was strong, and ranged from critical praise to a letter from one
Manitoba listener, who wrote, with glorious venom:

> What sort of insensitive clod would want to exploit the
> horrible burden carried by Robert Latimer and his wife
> every day? This reminds me of lines of a poem, "Stolid and
> stunned, a brother to an ox." …One of the quotes in the text
> was, "There is no joy in this for anyone." But the quote
> should have had this added to it: "Except for the CBC pro-
> ducer's promotion of this feeding frenzy."

The other advantage of dramatizing a real event, beyond the producer's apparent joy in exploiting misery, is that the parameters of
discussion can be enlarged. In the wake of the sentencing of Robert
Latimer, it is fair to say that the Canadian public was outraged, but
that anger seemed to stem from confusion and collateral events.
Latimer's sentence was cruelly long, particularly when weighed
against the simultaneous sentencing of Karla Homolka, who had
participated in the brutal murders of three young women. That a
father, acting from love and seeking to free a child from pain, would
have to serve an nearly identical amount of time with Homolka
enraged the public. There was also confusion with another high
profile case at that time, that of British Columbia's Sue Rodriguez.
Rodriguez, an adult afflicted with Lou Gehrig's disease, had made
a rational and eloquent appeal to be allowed the dignity of choosing

her own time of death. Lacking the ability to kill herself, Rodriguez requested an assisted suicide. In the Latimer case, the victim—a minor—had no say in the matter; the decision to die was made for her. And although I don't think there can be any question that Robert Latimer acted out of a profound, if misguided, love for his daughter, nevertheless his actions were murder, by our laws.

And it is that act of murder—which was obscured at the time by the outcry over Latimer's sentencing—that is examined most clearly and painfully in Sher's drama. Lost all along in the events were the voices of the disabled, many of whom felt profoundly threatened by Latimer's act, and the apparent majority support of him. Sher's sympathies ultimately reside with the child and he expressed them not in her voice—she was unable to speak—but through a new fictional character, Keith, a young man with Down's Syndrome. The portion of Sher's drama that most closely follows the Latimer case ends two-thirds of the way through the play, and it is at that point that Sher clearly begins working terrain that is close to him, and which is expressed most clearly when Keith disappears up the fire tower, afraid that what has been done to Tina will next be done to him.

In my notes to Sher I had initially suggested that if he meant to weigh in as an advocate for the disabled then he should do so earlier on in the drama. He resisted, and I now realize correctly so. The power of the final scenes on the firetower, when Doug must confront Keith—and after we have spent the majority of the drama in Doug's corner, as one does with the protagonist—is much stronger for having the tables finally turned.

KEITH:	She's dead.
DOUG:	She went to sleep and she never woke up.
KEITH:	She. She wasn't a dog.
DOUG:	No, she wasn't.
KEITH:	She was your daughter.
DOUG:	She still is.
KEITH:	She was my friend.
DOUG:	I know.
KEITH:	You killed her like she was a dog. It's what you do to dogs. You put them to sleep.

And immediately thereafter Sher employs a radio device—the repeated, reverbed bit of speech, to underline this moment of rawness, by quoting again the prosecutor's words:

CHISHOLM: *(Reverb/Courtroom.)* It is not open season on the disabled.

The ability to slide in those phrases proves the experience of Sher in the radio drama format. (In fact, he is now editor for the dramas that are aired on Morningside.) He's no slouch when using the tricks of the trade and, in *Mourning Dove*, blended both naturalistic and non-naturalistic elements.

Radio lends logic to time travel, and scenes that move rapidly back and forth through time are easily accomplished. Sher stays in the present and near past, moving from the trial and its aftermath backwards in time to the events that precipitated the tragedy. Originally he had had a third time layer to the story, flashbacks to the central character's and Keith's youth, but he decided that was a little too much time warping, and a tipping of the documentary nature into fiction.

Sher has used radio's ability to change locales at the drop of a sound cue, and the drama ranges from the austere sound of the courtroom, to the bustle of the diner with its chorus of townspeople, to the home of Doug—with its background breathing—to outdoor locales. The scene in the fire tower was originally set in a cave, which carries its own ambience, the inevitable, echoing water drip. However Sher decided that a firetower had a geographical logic, and Keith could defend it without the aid of fire-power. What was left out was a musicscape. This had the effect of rooting *Mourning Dove* thoroughly in the docudrama mode. And, as such it became one of the most potent and heart-rending hours to air on the current affairs *Morningside*.

A SCRIPT EDITOR SHOULDN'T HAVE FAVOURITES and of course I don't, but I have to admit that the arrival of new Judith Thompson draft creates a little frisson of anticipation in my airless office. Thompson is, arguably, English Canada's best playwright; certainly there are very few writers anywhere who can match the power and intensity of her work, its sheer ability to reach into one's guts and give them a good, hard twist. And added to that excitement is Thompson's habit of massively rewriting each draft; the script editor generally gets three plays for the price of one, as she progresses with panache to her final production draft.

My editorial relationship with Thompson began with my pet project of 1991, a special radio mini-series intended to coincide with the Second International Women's Playwrights Festival. Thompson was one of six women commissioned to write half hour episodes for the series (which was broadcast on *Morningside*) and she contributed *White Sand*, a mind-blowing look inside the psyche of the white power movement.

That mini-series whetted our department's appetite for international writers and, in particular, for playwrights from the Commonwealth, with their shared language and concerns. A Commonwealth series followed on *Stereodrama*, which in turn led to an ongoing series of exchanges with Radio New Zealand and, most importantly, the Australian Broadcasting Corporation (ABC). Primarily the exchange consisted of trading finished dramas (it being cheaper for us to air Australian dramas than it is to repeat our own— go figure). However, a new series of co-productions with both the British Broadcasting Corporation and ABC are in the works, and our producers are guest directing on each other's networks. In 1994 James Roy went to Australia to produce Louis Nowra's *The Moon of the Exploding Trees* and Perth-based David Britton, Head of ABC's radio drama unit, came to Toronto, to produce *Stop Talking Like That*.

Thompson's drama was an easy choice for this transcontinental tango. Her international reputation is comparable to Nowra's and there was even an intriguing link in her family tree; Thompson's maternal grandfather, F.M. Ford, was briefly the Prime Minister of Australia. Thompson's drama is also bicultural. Joanne, an anorexic outcast in her Thunder Bay high school, travels with her family to Australia for an extended stay with an aged grandparent. The child's parents hope that the change of climate and a new school will somehow propel Joanne back to physical and emotional health, but Australia is neither kind nor gentle. The young girl eventually goes on a tramp with her grandfather, from which neither will return.

Radio is the perfect medium for Thompson's careening story; not only does it allow us to leap oceans and climates, but the extra-dimensionality of, for example, a grandfather flying through the air escorted by a flock of birds becomes at once plausible and gripping because we the listeners are creating the image ourselves, using the raw materials Thompson has supplied. Radio drama is much like literature that way. A good novel takes me ages to read, because I am compelled to stop at every key image or event and imagine it. With Thompson I find myself constantly amazed at her effortless ability to drop that startling simile, "as restless as a shark", or create an entire metaphoric scene the surface of which only briefly conceals something altogether different, and more dramatic. For example, the grandfather has an aviary, a seemingly benign old-man type of pastime, but there are no innocent hobbies in Thompson's world.

FERGUS: I got in bad trouble for having this here aviary, love. See I didn't want to worry Maura with it, her so ill, laid up, so I postponed telling her, about the birds, you see. And then one day she came out in her nightie, fancied a passionfruit, I suppose, and she heard the racket. Well she opened the shed doors and three hundred birds flew at her all at once and she dropped to a faint. Broke both her hips. Well she was not pleased, not a bit.

The listener creates the image. Maura is lying on Australian lawn— is it green or sunbaked? Is she in pain or lying in wide-eyed shock? Are the besieging birds exotic parrots or brightly coloured budgies? And so on; the radio drama becomes a kind of aural IKEA—all parts; a few Allen keys are supplied and the listener does the rest. The listener becomes co-creator with Judith Thompson, and the stronger the raw materials, the greater the ownership, and hence power of the piece.

Stop Talking Like That is hard work for the listener—and therefore more rewarding—because Thompson is not content to just make us work scenically—she wanders in and out of character's minds at the drop of a sound cue. The young girl who suffers so much in this play is not separated from us physically—there are no intervening seats, no coughs, no audience presence; we just have a quick ticket to the inside of her head. As with Hoda, the central character in Rachel Wyatt's *Crackpot*, Joanne's thoughts are given an undistracted point of entry courtesy of radio. So when Joanne muses to herself, "Baby, wherever are you going? I think I'll see you there. I think I will", we think it too.

Throughout the play, the mythic shares air with the mundane. The schoolyard talk of the young girls clashes with a sound bed that emphasizes mystery. When Joanne goes climbing with her grandfather we are clearly imagining her frail white limbs as she scrabbles up the rock and this, and her subsequent dangerous ride with the trucker, are clear, naturalistic images. But then, one sound cue later, her grandfather is flown off (and we're flying with him) and we're in an entirely new reality.

                    (In the Dream Time. Sound: FERGUS flying…
                    whooshing through the air like a great bird, plus
                    flute.)

FERGUS: *(Interior.)* Oh this is everything I imagined, this van-
                    ishing, flying, over desert, flying free, just like the
                    dreams, what a terrible weight a human body was,
                    a terrible…

                    (Sound: FERGUS' birds from the aviary—a great
                    clamour.)

                    My friends from the shed, hullo, hullo, my lovely
                    birdies how good of you to come and guide me to
                    wherever I'm going wherever…

GEORGE F. WALKER is the other English Canadian playwright
with an international presence to match that of Thompson. His work
has been performed at theatres around the world and, like Thompson,
he has also worked in film and television. I think Walker is drawn
to radio drama because of the artistic freedom it offers him—there
are not those multitudes of script doctors and hangers-on who
reduce most of film and television to pap and drive fiercely inde-
pendent writers like Walker to distraction. And there is certainly a
lot less hassle in having a play produced for radio than for stage—
once a commission is made, matters progress quickly. The actual
script creation process can proceed at the playwright's pace, which
in Walker's case is rapid.

Walker has not historically written much for radio, but that is
now changing. *How To Make Love To An Actor* is the first of a trilogy
of radio plays; the second part (which was broadcast in the fall of
1996) is subtitled *The Green Room* and it does to theatre what *How To
Make Love to an Actor* did to the film business.

As a general rule, we have an aversion to producing plays "on
the trade". The temptation for everyone who has ever been involved
in theatre is intense at some point in their career to exorcise demons,
settle past scores or simply describe the absurdities of that most
wonderful of all professions. The trouble is, it often gets too far
inside, especially for a national audience which is definitely outside
the theatre world. But Walker is an equal opportunity satirist;
everyone gets nailed and it's a kind of universal pillaging. For
example, the pretentiousness of moviespeak is exposed when Ross
the slasher film producer outlines his inspirations.

ROSS: ...Do you know the sources I drew on for this
                   thing? They're classic. Classic sources. Greek!
                   They're Greek! And they're Shakespearean. Big
                   Greek Shakespearean sources not to mention the
                   Catholics. Scorsese and Coppola and Pasolini and
                   all those other great Catholic guys and their sources
                   about mothers and Jonathan's prototypes and the
                   classic hate love beauty sex death punishment guilt
                   violence redemption panorama...

But hold on, theatre gets it as well.

SANDY: You're a political person, aren't you.

JESS: What's that supposed to mean.

SANDY: It means you've got a point of view or something.
                   You do a lot of small theatre work, don't you?

JESS: Yeah. So?

SANDY: So that probably explains your point of view.

JESS: Which is?

SANDY: Limited.

And even playwrights get it. In fact, only dramaturges are axempted;
either Walker has had an exceptionally charmed and untheory-
beset career, or he is saving up a whole play for them.
    Radiophonically, *How to Make Love to an Actor* is quite close to a
stage play and, indeed, could be staged with just a few changes in the
blocking. The closeness to stage presents some dangers. The play is
moving in real time but some events—the shower scene in particular—happen with magic efficiency, especially in light of how much
liquor has been consumed. Walker deals with the incongruity head
on, and gets away with it, on charm alone. Jess is offstage for about
sixty seconds and then she returns:

JESS: *(Moving on.)* I threw up. I had a fast shower. I bor-
                   rowed your bathrobe, Willie. I borrowed your
                   toothbrush. I feel better.

I suppose what Walker's script does is prove that good writing will work regardless of the medium. Radio does many things well and some things better than stage—changing locales at the drop of the sound cue being the prominent example—but Walker has ignored all the little bonuses radio offers up, and made his play succeed on the basis of its fast moving plot, fascinating characters and, above all, scintillating dialogue.

Walker's writing process is almost the opposite to Thompson's: whereas the latter will radically alter each draft, Walker's first draft is almost letter perfect. In his case, most of my notes dealt with entrances and exits, helping with transitions between the scenes. I had worried a lot about the fight scenes—they are almost always problematic on radio—unless there are snippets of dialogue it is sometimes hard to tell exactly who is getting the worst of things. Walker solved this by inserting an astonishing amount of dialogue amidst the flying bodies.

JESS: *(A loud sustained scream as she comes running on and attacks ROSS.)*

(Sound: Things being knocked over.)

Hey God. It's me. The bug. Make me an offer!

(Sound: Body hitting the floor.)

ROSS: Hey get off me. Get away. Ouch! Hey stop! Hey, man. You're kicking me... Hey! ow...

JESS: Make me an offer. Come on make me an offer.

(Biz: She kicks him.)

And so on. It's a great fight, with lots for the ear. There is more conflict in a half minute of Walker's piece than in the entire fifty-four minutes of *The Mercy Quilt*—which illustrates again the flexibility of radio—both work.

Finally, I had been worried that the scenes where two or more characters speak for prolonged periods would make terrible radio, but in actualily, the effect was to force the listener to adopt one of the speakers and follow his or her speech. And to bring them back to catch the repeat broadcast the next evening on *Monday Night Playhouse*...

RACHEL WYATT HAS BEEN CALLED THE QUEEN of radio drama and she is the most experienced playwright currently working in radio in this country. The author of more than 130 radio dramas, Wyatt was the ideal choice for the difficult task of dramatizing Adele Wiseman's second novel *Crackpot*. Wiseman had won the Governor General's Award for her first novel, *The Sacrifice*, and her follow-up book (after an eighteen year interval) marked the creation of one of the great characters of Canadian fiction, Hoda. Fat, ill-educated, daughter of a blind widower, spurned by her relatives, Hoda should have been marked for disaster, but instead she lives her life in reverse—her early traumas gradually giving way to small victories, won by her cheerful and indomitable character and her insistence on exercising control over her life even as chaos closes in on her. When her rich relatives will not support Hoda and her father, she discovers that turning tricks can pay the rent. She fools her father by saying the money flowing in is coming for the baskets he weaves—and, in fact, her johns must take one basket per visit. Hoda also follows politics, with an intellectual support for workers' rights, but an emotional fixation with royalty and, in particular, the Prince of Wales. When she gives birth to a child and must identify a father—there are many candidates—she turns to this fantasy realm, naming the prince. She sends her child to an orphanage, but Winnipeg is a small enough city to ensure that Hoda will once again meet her son.

I read *Crackpot* right after its publication in 1974 and never forgot the novel and, in particular, Hoda. When Adele Wiseman died in 1992 I wondered if there wasn't some way we could honour her life by bringing the novel to radio. A fortuitous encounter with Wyatt revealed that she knew Wiseman, and the project was born. The resulting drama is one of the best we've ever aired—a magnificent sweeping play that captures all that is wonderful about the novel and Hoda. It has been the CBC nominee for a number of international awards, and a stage adaptation by Rachel is currently having international success.

Novel dramatizations are a tricky business. Often there is too much reverence on the part of the dramatist for the author and subject matter which, when coupled with the playwright's own relationship with the novelist (and the script editor's passion for the book), can lead to the urge to include absolutely everything in the dramatization. And then there is the question of literariness, which must be purged—long glorious description not being quite so engaging when off the page. (Although, as I write this I can immediately think of two stunning exceptions, David Young's dramatizations of Michael Ondaatje's *The Skin of the Lion* and *The English Patient*.) Novels also tend not to have a dramatic structure and often run a bit weak on dialogue which, in radio drama, must contain virtually all of the information for the listener, unless some kind of conscious or unconscious narrative voice is used. And if the latter course is taken, the temptation immediately becomes nearly irresistible to narrate great chunks.

On the other hand, a novel arrives at the dramatist's door with a story ready-made, and radio is above all a storytelling medium. The hour-long format of *Sunday Showcase* and *Monday Night Playhouse* requires a strong current of plot to keep the listener from wandering off (to do the dishes). We get hundreds of submissions every year and I sometimes lapse into despair at the apparent inability of many playwrights to assemble even a relatively slim story. A number of writers seem to mistake a good idea—or an intriguing pose—as the kind of dramatic content that can retain the interest of a listener. There are any number of theories as to why this has come to pass; perhaps that the art of storytelling has indeed fallen into intellectual disrepute as an unnatural, contrived exercise. But I also suspect there are other forces at work, not the least of which is our shortening attention span. Most of us have now grown up with our chief storytelling influence being the twenty-four minute sitcom or, more recently, the three minute video. In any event, without "story", the ephemerality of radio can easily fade the most inventive drama into ether. Which is not to say that experimental dramas haven't worked in the medium; I just can't think of any recent examples. I look forward to the exception.

Ultimately the listener—as with the reader—wants to know what happens next. It's a rhythm of consciousness as innate as our desire to understand what happened before. And unlike novels—which can be placed on end tables when they frustrate, and picked up later—the radio gets turned off. And when that little bit of air disappears into time, it's well and truly gone.

Crackpot the novel had story and Wyatt the dramatist made it scenic. She began with a teaser, a kind of montage of voices. My father used to give speeches a lot and he said the main thing you had to do was start with a "ho-hum crasher". (He said you were supposed to end with one too. There was no advice about the middle—I think it was filler. Just as well I'm the one script editing.) In any event, Wyatt managed in the space of this quick montage to pose a number of questions that the listener immediately wanted answered, answers for which they would stay tuned for the entire hour.

> *(Prologue. All these voices are remote, tangential. Some more remote than others.)*

HODA: Tell me the story, Daddy.

DANILE: You wouldn't believe our luck. For on the surface, aren't we the unluckiest people on the earth?

VOICES: Hoda! Hoda! Fat pig, Hoda. Crackpot, Hoda!

MOTHER: What were you and your friends playing out in the shed, Hoda?

HODA: Doctors and nurses, Ma.

DANILE: Miracle! Our little girl wants to be a doctor.

HODA: I like being the patient too, Daddy...

Wyatt avoided the use of narrator, though she did employ two other tricks. She allowed Hoda's inner voice to be heard periodically. This allows the listener into the head of the outcast Hoda and, assuming that the listener is not an obese prostitute from Winnipeg, it's as close as we can get to the psyche of someone whom we might instinctively cross the street to avoid.

HODA: He said I love you. He didn't mean it. I could tell. He only said it 'cause I told him to. *(Beat.)* We could sure use the money. But I did it. Did I really do it? Is that what it's all about? Will they know? Will people be able to tell? Can they see from my face? *(Beat.)* It felt good. Felt really good.

Wyatt also introduced a chorus of women, a clever device for sneaking out chunks of exposition in a humorous way, and also give a sense of Hoda's isolation and the community mores she was flouting.

GUSIA: She goes to every wedding.

MRS. LETZ: Eats the best food.

MRS. POLONICK: Comes to my daughter's wedding. No invitation. So they ask her which side and she says, bold as brass, "Both sides, I'm a friend."

GUSIA: Now they look for her. It's not a proper wedding without Hoda. She brings luck.

MRS. LETZ: Luck! She eats like a vacuum cleaner and they say what she does with the ushers outside...

MRS.
POLONICK: Once even the groom!

Wyatt's experience shows in some of her sound instructions. Her first scene opens with this instruction as to street noise: "The outside street sounds are of pedestrians, horse-drawn vehicles—but this isn't a through street…") And if you stop to think of it she has a point—traffic does move differently on a through street. Another favourite instruction comes much later when Wyatt specifies that footsteps must "crunch" in the snow—this plays into one of our great communal pools of knowledge, that a particular snow sound can tell us how cold it is.

Throughout she has also used sound to continue the montages, the reverberated sounds of the past and even ends with Hoda's life played back. It provides a bracket to the opening teaser, a summing up, and Wyatt ends it with a sly homage to Hoda's creator. Hoda is lying in bed beside her new husband, marvelling that she has never before spent an entire night with a man.

> *(LAZAR snores lightly again. Dream music. Hints of violins, Royal wedding, marching band. In dream from now to end.)*

HODA: I've got to remember this when I wake up.

> *(Sound: Wreckers knocking down a building.)*

That's the orphanage. They're tearing it down. Here little Danny. Stand by me. Something I have to tell you. Cherish your corpses. They give your life body.

GUSIA: Crackpot Hoda. Have respect.

POLONICK: A heroine, Hoda.

DAVID: *(In wonder.)* You lived your life backwards, mother.

HODA: See now, I curtsey to you all. To you, Prince, to you Duchess, to you poor Uncle, to you and you…

> *(Music up to end.)*

LAZAR: Sleep gently, Hoda.

DANILE: My father, though only a tailor by trade, was a wise man…

IF I WAS A PESSIMIST, I'd tell you that this could well be the last anthology of radio drama. The CBC continues to get slammed with funding cuts and radio performance is taking its share of hits. The number of drama programs has diminished in the past couple of years, both in the number of new dramas produced and in the loss entire programs. Radio drama is expensive—though no more so than current affairs documentaries—and it can be controversial, which is not necessarily viewed as a plus in these timid corporate times.

But I'm an optimist, and I have to believe that this unique form of drama is going to outlast the current era of cutbacks. When radio drama is good it's disturbing, and when it sets about creating a world in the air it can be a place as big as our brains. The form grows more fascinating to me with each passing year. In fact, I think of all the performing arts it might well be the one which invites the most intelligent and participatory response. And if that sounds like a theory, well then I'll be damned, aurally.

Dave Carley
Toronto, 1996

THE MERCY QUILT

LORRE JENSEN

Lorre Jensen was born in Toronto, spent her early childhood years at Tyendinega Mohawk Territory and her school years at The Mohawk Institute in Brantford. She has lived in Toronto for all of her adult life and comes to playwriting after a twenty year career in advertising and television production.

Her plays include *Coming Around,* co-written with Paula Wing, for Theatre New Brunswick's Young People's Theatre; *Pen Pals,* a drama about the lives and deaths of women in prison; *The Shaman of Waz,* a Native musical-comedy based on *The Wizard of Oz,* and *The Mercy Quilt.*

The playwright gratefully acknowledges the assistance of the Toronto Arts Council, the Ontario Arts Council and The Canada Council, whose grants made much of her writing possible.

The Mercy Quilt was first broadcast on *Sunday Showcase*, on Sunday, January 5, 1997, with the following cast:

GRACE .... Carol Greyeyes

MARGE .... Pamela Matthews

LORRAINE .... Columpa Bobb

MAY .... Sandra LaRonde

WANDA .... Gail Maurice

SARAH .... Gloria Eshkibok

CARL and EARL .... Dennis O'Connor

POLICEMAN and CASHIER .... Wayne Robson

OLD DAVEY .... Ron Cook

Producer .... Lynda Hill

Associate Producer .... Sandra Jeffries-Broitman

Recording Engineer .... Greg DeClute

Sound Effects .... John Stewart

Executive Producer .... James Roy

Casting Director .... Linda Grearson

Script Editor .... Dave Carley

*Dedicated to the memory of Marge Hill,
an aunt, friend, elder and role model.*

Scene One

(Outdoors. Sound: Native drumming and singing from a distance, jingling from bells comes closer, then fades. Sound: Laughter, children calling, general exterior crowd sounds. Establish, then fade under:)

MARGE: So many people! Oh, Grace, this Pow-Wow's brought home so many old faces.

GRACE: I'll say. And a lot of them old faces were young the last time we saw them. I can hardly make out who they were when they left.

MARGE: Well, they're home again. That's what counts. And we're all together. It's just like old times. Puts me in mind of when we were girls, doing all that fancing dancing with our shawls.

GRACE: Maybe we can go round once or twice when they sing a slow one, Marge. Just for old times' sake.

MARGE: You'll have to dance for both of us, Grace.

GRACE: Oh, I don't know if I could go round four times.

MARGE: Your girl's coming, Grace. Lorraine'll dance with you tomorrow.

GRACE: These are happy days, ain't they, Marge? Days like these make you want to go on forever.

MARGE: Grace! Who's that waving at us?

GRACE: It's the undertaker! What's he doing here? Marge, pinch me.

MARGE: What for?

GRACE: Pinch me! I want to be sure he's not coming for me.

MARGE: *(Calling out.)* Carl! Carl!

GRACE: You don't have to call him, Marge. He'll be coming for us soon enough.

MARGE: Grace, I don't know what gets into you. I'm going to sell Carl a ticket.

CARL: Hello, Marge, Grace. Well, this is quite a crowd, a, a gathering! And everybody's dressed up. Looks like a regular Mardi Gras.

MARGE: It's our Pow-Wow, Carl. First one we've had in years.

CARL: First one I've ever seen. In person, I mean. Where'd everybody come from?

GRACE: They're all our relations.

CARL: Really? I heard some of them came from Wisconsin.

GRACE: They're distant relations.

MARGE: Can we sell you a ticket, Carl? They're only a dollar apiece and this here's the prize. Make a nice gift.

              (Sound: Muted sound of a turtle rattle coming from the beads.)

CARL: Oh yeah? I was hoping you'd be raffling another quilt this year.

GRACE: Ain't too many of us left who can quilt all day, Carl. You took most of them away.

MARGE: That's got nothing to do with Carl.

GRACE: They're dead, ain't they?

MARGE: Don't mind, Grace. You had your heart set on winning a quilt, did you, Carl?

CARL: Yeah, kind of. I've been telling my sister all about your quilts. I know she'd like one. She was asking if you had any for sale.

MARGE: Well, if she don't mind waiting a little. We never quilt till after the first snowfall. You could give the beads to her, Carl.

CARL: Let's have a look at them.

MARGE: Here. Ain't they something?

CARL: Yes, Ma'am. Very unusual.

(Sound: Muted turtle rattle continues under:)

MARGE: Special order, that's why.

CARL: So, so blue. What do you call that? It's not royal blue.

MARGE: Wanda Shewanda calls it the colour of summer twilight. She's the one that made them.

GRACE: It's for a good cause, you know. All the money's going for our new museum. Marge, you tell him we went all the way to Manitoulin Island? Got them direct from the artist. What do you think of the turtle in the middle?

CARL: Yeah! It's a nice touch. Looks real, doesn't it?

GRACE: Hand carved, that's why. Turtles mean a lot to us. Always have.

CARL: Well, you sold me. And look, if I win, I'll give them to you, for your new museum. When's the draw?

MARGE: Two weeks today. We're giving a tea at the Elders' Lodge.

GRACE: Say, look at them kids up there, dancing to beat the band. Carl, you ever do any dancing like that?

CARL: No, Grace, I've barely mastered the box step.

MARGE: Go ahead and join in, Carl. It's for everybody.

CARL: Oh, it is? Okay, I'll, I'll…try.

(Calling back.)

Wish me luck!

MARGE:	*(Calling.)* Watch the others.
GRACE:	The box step? Never heard of it. Must be talking about square dancing.
MARGE:	Now where's Sarah? She's supposed to spell us. Go and find her, Grace.
GRACE:	You should go, Marge. The exercise'll do you good.
MARGE:	Somebody's got to mind the beads.
GRACE:	Let's flip for it.
MARGE:	She's coming now. *(Calls.)* Sarah!
SARAH:	I'm coming. It's this new hip. I'm not used to it yet.
GRACE:	Where's Kathleen? I suppose she forgot.
SARAH:	I just reminded her. Kathleen, I said, it's our turn to sell the tickets.
MARGE:	We might have to go after her again. Everything slips her mind nowdays.
SARAH:	You go on. I'm gonna sit here and enjoy this Pow-Wow. Sure brings back a lot of memories.
	(CAST & Sound: Drumming, singing grows and then fade.)

Scene Two

(MARGE's front porch. Music: Solo flute. Sound: Exterior night-time sounds: crickets, water gently lapping at shoreline.)

MARGE:	What's keeping that girl of yours, Grace?
GRACE:	Hard to believe she's coming home. And for good this time. Never has to leave again.
MARGE:	Lorraine's been gone a long time.
GRACE:	Thirty years.

SARAH: Thirty years! Hmm. Seems like yesterday you sent her off on the train. She was just a girl. Going so far away. So fearless. You know who she puts me in mind of?

(Music: Flute plays a 'signature' flourish.)

Handsome. He was like that.

GRACE: Everything puts you in mind of Handsome, Sarah. I s'pose an old soup pot would put you in mind of Handsome.

SARAH: Feels good to think about him, Grace. Now, where did I put my pipe? Here it is.

(Sound: Matches being struck and puffing sounds will continue under:)

GRACE: Sarah looks just like Mammy Yokum with that pipe, don't she, Marge?

MARGE: Don't pay her no mind. You think it's good to be smoking like that?

SARAH: Handsome smoked this pipe every day of his life. Never hurt him none. Smoking it puts me in mind of him. *(Sucking on pipe.)*

(Music: Flute plays 'Handsome' signature.)

I don't inhale.

MARGE: Well, if it keeps his memory alive—

SARAH: I'm glad I got memories. You take poor Kathleen. All her memories are hiding somewheres. Locked away in her bank and she don't remember what she done with the key.

MARGE: She's got her health.

GRACE: All her own parts, too, Sarah. None of them silicon hips.

(Sound: Yapping of a small dog.)

MARGE: Someone's coming.

SARAH: I got to get me a watchdog like yours, Marge.

MARGE: I hope it's Lorraine.

                (Sound: Engine sounds as car approaches.)

SARAH: That dog's got special powers.

                (Sound: Engine shuts off, car door opens and closes, footsteps up the stairs.)

GRACE: It's my girl.

LORRAINE: Hah! The whole gang's here. Hi, Aunt Marge, Sarah. Hi, Ma!

                (Biz: A loud kiss.)

                Hmm. It's good to be home.

SARAH: Ain't you a sight! And just as slim as ever.

GRACE: Just as single, too.

                (Sound: LORRAINE plops into chair.)

LORRAINE: Ma, you make it sound like a disease.

MARGE: Now, Grace, marriage isn't for everybody.

GRACE: Back in our day, Marge, if you didn't get married, you got left behind. Folks thought there was something wrong with you.

LORRAINE: There must be something wrong with me. Maybe it's a social disease, eh, Ma?

GRACE: There ain't nothing wrong with you. That's what I can't understand.

MARGE: Oh, Grace, I'm sure Lorraine had the chance.

LORRAINE: I did.

GRACE: What happened?

LORRAINE: Ah, Ma.

MARGE: She just wants to know you've been asked, is all,

Lorraine. You picked a good time to come home. We're having a big dance. It's going on all weekend.

LORRAINE: Yeah! The joint's really jumping, eh? About time we had a Pow-Wow around here.

GRACE: Our tickets are gonna go like hot-cakes.

LORRAINE: You got another raffle going, Ma?

GRACE: Yup. And we got a good prize, too.

MARGE: Wait, Grace. Start at the beginning.

GRACE: You tell it, Marge.

MARGE: We started a museum. It's gonna be up at the Elders' Lodge. Because we got all these things from the past, packed away. Sarah's even got wampum.

SARAH: Found it in the attic. Belonged to my grandmother.

MARGE: We're gonna put it on show and let everybody see it. So we figured it'd be a good idea to have some cases made, you know, to display everything. Isaac's making them. He made all them tables at the council house.

GRACE: He's handy like that, Lorraine. He's a widower, you know.

MARGE: Oh, Grace! He's too old for Lorraine. He's eighty-five if he's a day!

LORRAINE: That'd be carbon dating, Ma.

GRACE: He's good at cards. Comes every week, with a loaf of egg sandwiches for the lunch. Even cuts off the crusts!

LORRAINE: He doesn't appear to need a wife.

SARAH: Grace, you oughta run one of them matchmaking outfits.

GRACE: Could be a match made in heaven.

LORRAINE: Ma, Isaac's halfway to heaven as it is and it's not from being lovestruck.

SARAH: Go on, Marge. Tell Lorraine about them cupboards. Before Grace's got her married off to Father Time.

MARGE: Gonna be our gift. From the whole club.

LORRAINE: The quilting club?

MARGE: That's right. There's Sarah and me your Ma and—

LORRAINE: What about Kathleen?

MARGE: Kathleen's getting awful…forgetful.

GRACE: Tell Lorraine about the tickets, Marge.

MARGE: I'm getting to it, Grace. We got a prize that kinda fits right in with the museum.

GRACE: Went all the way to Manitoulin Island to get it too.

LORRAINE: Who went to Manitoulin Island?

GRACE: We did.

LORRAINE: Who took you?

GRACE: We took ourselves!

SARAH: That's where we met Wanda Shewanda.

LORRAINE: Never heard of her.

SARAH: She's a born artist, if you ask me. Puts me in mind of Handsome.

                    (Music: Flute plays the 'Handsome' signature.)

SARAH: He was always making something. She made the beads. Even carved a little turtle to go in the middle.

LORRAINE: The beads are the prize, I take it.

MARGE: We drove a good bargain for them. Show Lorraine the beads, Sarah.

SARAH: I gave them to Kathleen.

(*Music: Can underscore this calamity. Possibly "Oh, Oh".*)

MARGE: Oh, Sarah!

GRACE: No telling what will become of them.

SARAH: It's just for tonight, Marge.

GRACE: They'll be gone the way of the dodo bird. (*Voice trailing off.*) Probably forgot where they laid their eggs, just disappeared.

Scene Three

(*MARGE's front room. Music: Flute begins and punctuates the pauses in the telephone call.*)

MARGE: Kathleen, it's the blue beads we got from Wanda Shewanda. The prize. (*Pause.*) The beads Sarah gave you to mind. (*Pause.*) Are you sure you don't have them? (*Pause.*)

(*Sound: Rhythmic tapping at the door.*)

She's at the door now. I'll ask her. We'll see you at the dance.

(*Sound: Telephone tone, then receiver is clicked. The door opens.*)

Scene Four

(*MARGE's front room.*)

GRACE: Anybody home? Marge?

(*CAST: General hubbub of "gang" arriving.*)

LORRAINE: You talk to Kathleen?

MARGE: She can't remember the beads at all.

GRACE: Does she remember the Pow-Wow?

MARGE: Oh, yes.

SARAH: Did you ask her to look around?

MARGE: She wouldn't know what she was looking for.

GRACE: I knew it.

MARGE: She didn't even know what I was talking about. Sarah, are you sure you gave them to her?

SARAH: Course, I'm sure! She had that big old purse look like a feed sack. I said, "Kathleen, put these in your purse while I count the money."

MARGE: You ask her, Sarah. Act out how you gave them to her.

SARAH: I can't.

LORRAINE: Why can't you?

SARAH: See, this thing about forgetting, she tries to hide it. Makes excuses, like, to cover up. We can't keep after her about it.

LORRAINE: We may have to look ourselves.

GRACE: You mean go through her purse?

LORRAINE: No, Ma. I mean go through her house.

MARGE: We'll need a search warrant. I've seen that on teevee.

LORRAINE: Is Kathleen going to the Pow-Wow?

MARGE: I told her we'd meet her there.

LORRAINE: Then she won't be home. I'll go to her house. Ma, you come as look out.

GRACE: I want no part of it. It's against the law.

MARGE: It could get us all in the slammer. I've seen that on teevee.

SARAH: You're right, Marge. The police'll take a dim view of that.

LORRAINE: They'll be up at the Pow-Wow like everybody else.
               Crowd control. Even if they do drive by, what will
               they think? They know you, Ma. We won't be
               wearing masks.

GRACE: That's what worries me. I might faint. They'll know
               we're up to no good.

LORRAINE: You won't faint, Ma.

GRACE: We should flip for it, Marge.

MARGE: It's these old legs of mine. What if we had to make
               a run for it? I've seen that on teevee.

GRACE: What about you, Sarah?

LORRAINE: Sarah's just got a new hip.

SARAH: I don't know what Handsome's going to make of all
               this.

LORRAINE: Look, Ma. If Kathleen was sick, wouldn't you go in,
               even if you had to break down the door?

GRACE: Course, I would.

LORRAINE: Well, she is sick, in a way.

GRACE: But she won't be there.

LORRAINE: That's why we're going in. What's wrong, Ma?

GRACE: It's double talk. You sound just like an Indian
               agent.

LORRAINE: Look! If she was there, and we went barging in to
               look for the beads, after she said she didn't have
               them, she would be hurt.

GRACE: You figure she won't be hurt?

LORRAINE: She won't know. We have to look, Ma. Think about
               the Museum. You'd be doing it for a good cause.

GRACE: Well… I s'pose we'll need a ruse.

MARGE: Take a pie, Grace. Makes a good alibi.

SARAH: Stick it in the oven. Act like you're baking it.

GRACE: Which one should I take?

SARAH: Take the rhubarb, Grace.

Scene Five

(Outside KATHLEEN's house. Sound: Turning of door handle, followed by the exertion of pushing at it.)

LORRAINE: Funny. The door's locked.

GRACE: Let's go.

LORRAINE: Here, Ma. Hold my purse.

GRACE: I'm holding the pie.

LORRAINE: Put the pie down. Here.

(Sound: Purse being opened and a fumble through the contents.)

GRACE: What are you doing?

LORRAINE: It's a simple lock. I think I can get in with a credit card.

GRACE: You learn that in the city?

LORRAINE: Yeah. Okay. That's got it.

(Sound: Door handle turning, door opening.)

Scene Six

(Interior of KATHLEEN's house. Sound: Door closing. Footsteps.)

GRACE: Oh, my! Kathleen got a new—

LORRAINE: Ma, you watch at the window.

(Sound: Footsteps on tile.)

GRACE: What about the pie?

LORRAINE: Put it in the oven.

(Sound: Oven door opening and closing.)

GRACE: Should I turn it on?

LORRAINE: No.

GRACE: Well, how will we bake it?

LORRAINE: We're just pretending.

GRACE: It would look better with the oven on.

LORRAINE: Turn it on low then. Ma, stand by the window as lookout.

(Sound: Footsteps trailing away.)

GRACE: Somebody might see me.

LORRAINE: They'll think it's Kathleen. I'll look around.

GRACE: *(Calling.)* Lorraine!

(Sound: Muffled sound of hurried footsteps.)

LORRAINE: Somebody coming?

GRACE: No. Look at this!

(Sound: Footsteps on tile.)

LORRAINE: What?

(Sound: Refrigerator door being opened.)

GRACE: She's got eight pounds of butter in here. What's she doing with all that butter?

LORRAINE: Why are you looking in her fridge?

GRACE: I always look in the fridge when I'm nervous.

(Sound: Fridge door closes, followed by muffled

footsteps which will continue under along with ambient searching sounds.)

LORRAINE: Check in her desk, Ma.

GRACE: She's got private things in there. We shoulda got May to look for the beads.

LORRAINE: Why?

GRACE: Cause May's Kathleen's girl. May would know right where to look. S'pose May walked in the door right now? We didn't think of that.

LORRAINE: Oh, Ma. Don't say that.

GRACE: Here's a picture of Isaac right by the bed. She must be carrying on with him.

LORRAINE: Oh, Geez, Ma, why are we here?

GRACE: To bake the pie?

LORRAINE: NO!

GRACE: If anybody asks why we're here, we're baking the pie.

LORRAINE: Good. Keep looking.

GRACE: Stuck on Isaac! I'd a thought them genes a hers be pretty wore out by now.

LORRAINE: Ma, don't say anything to the others. That's private.

GRACE: It was your idea to break into her house. But…we did it together. That's important.

LORRAINE: I can't find the beads. Let's get out of here.

                (Sound: Door opening.)

GRACE: We broke the law for nothing.

LORRAINE: There's the satisfaction that we looked.

GRACE: It don't seem right coming away empty-handed after breaking in.

                (Sound: Door closing behind them.)

Scene Seven

> *(Outside KATHLEEN's house. Sound: Exterior ambience, footsteps on gravel, door closing and click of lock.)*

GRACE: The pie!

LORRAINE: We'll have to leave it, Ma. The door's locked. I don't want to break in again.

GRACE: But Kathleen will find it.

LORRAINE: She'll think she baked it.

GRACE: We should have brought pumpkin.

LORRAINE: Why?

GRACE: It's her favourite.

Scene Eight

> *(The local IGA store. Sound: Background clatter, slight clanging of metal carts and cash register bells.)*

CASHIER: Hi, Sarah!

SARAH: You got any of that Daily Mail pipe tobacco?

CASHIER: Let me check. It's probably in the back.

MAY: Sarah! Why aren't you at the Pow-Wow?

> *(Sound: Muted turtle rattle continues under:)*

SARAH: Just come from there, May. Got to get my, my...my...

MAY: What's wrong, Sarah?

SARAH: My! ...Those are nice beads you got on.

MAY: Thanks. Ma gave them to me.

SARAH: Kathleen? Gave them to you?

MAY: Uh huh! Right out of the blue. For my birthday, she said. Are you alright? You look pale.

SARAH: For your birthday. It's nice that she remembered.

MAY: I was kinda hoping for a pair of hip waders.

SARAH: Hip waders?

MAY: For fishing.

SARAH: You fish, do you?

MAY: Every day. Rain or shine.

SARAH: I got to be going. *(Voice trails off.)* Nice seeing you, May.

(Sound: Rattle fades.)

CASHIER: *(Calling.)* Sarah! Wait. Your tobacco!

Scene Nine

(Pow-Wow grounds. Music: Flute threads its way through. CAST/Sound: Exterior crowd, laughter. Chatter, children, jingling of bells.)

GRACE: There's Kathleen now. Dancing like she hasn't a care in the world. Looks like a swirling dervish. Funny she don't forget how to dance, eh, Marge?

MARGE: Can you see if she's wearing the beads?

GRACE: No. She's wearing...looks like a string of popcorn. Wonder what she done with the beads.

MARGE: You sure you looked everywhere, Grace?

GRACE: We turned the place inside out. Just like on teevee.

MARGE: You straighten up when you were done?

LORRAINE: We had to leave the pie, Aunt Marge.

MARGE: Well, it's always nice to take a little something when you go visiting. Listen. it looks like Old Davey is going to make a speech. This dance was his idea, Lorraine.

GRACE: He sits in that rocker up at the Elders'. Never says a word. Half the time it's hard to tell if he's still with us. So shy, he can hardly bid at cards. Then, one night, he pipes up about having a dance.

MARGE: He give a good talk about all the things we're forgetting. Don't know where he found the words.

GRACE: Must be the ones he's been saving for so long.

                (Sound: Screeching of microphone being tested. General crowd sound fades; only the odd jingling of bells is heard throughout this speech.)

OLD DAVEY: Sek:on! Can everybody hear?

                (CAST/General applause and the sounds of a large gathering coming to order. A cough, a child's giggles shushed.)

                Sek:on! I just want to say a few words, to count my blessings out loud, in front of everybody, that all our people are together again visiting with one another and giving thanks. When my grandmother was a young girl, that's a long time ago, we had a lotta dances throughout the year, when we planted the corn, then when it was getting ripe, and when we harvested the corn. Lotta dances. And ceremonies for the berries, for the sun and for thunder, to bring the rain, to make the crops grow. Somehow, we forgot all this. And it pretty near disappeared. Then we pretty near disappeared. It got so we couldn't make out who we were. As a people. That's why we got to keep the dances going, to pay our respects to all the grandparents. Cause if we just go on forgetting, we'll have nothing to give to the children.

                (CAST/Sound: Lavish applause and whistles, crowd and jingle noises continue under. Clapping gently fades until one pair of hands is heard.)

MARGE: Davey should run for chief.

Scene Ten

                *(The Pow-Wow grounds. Music: Flute is present
                and drum beats in background. Sound/biz:
                Footsteps running, SARAH panting.)*

SARAH: *(Breathing hard.)* You'll never guess who I saw
                down at the IGA!

MARGE: Sarah! You look like you saw a ghost.

GRACE: Was it Handsome?

SARAH: May! That's who. Kathleen's girl. She was wearing
                the beads.

MARGE: Are you sure?

SARAH: I know the beads when I see them.

GRACE: Did you tell her they were ours?

SARAH: No, Grace.

MARGE: Sarah, what did you say?

SARAH: Nothing. I was shocked, like. She saw me staring at
                them. She said, "Ma gave them to me. Right out of
                the blue!"

GRACE: What else?

SARAH: Said something about going fishing. I must have
                left the tobacco at the IGA.

LORRAINE: I'm going to tell May. I'll just say that Kathleen
                forgot and—

MARGE: No, Lorraine. That's not a good idea.

LORRAINE: Why not, Aunt Marge?

MARGE: There's no mercy in it. It'll give away Kathleen's
                secret and disappoint May at the same time. We got

to come up with a plan that saves everybody's feelings.

SARAH: Let's think on it while we watch the dances. Maybe after a while, we'll come up with something.

OLD DAVEY: *(Faint voice, calling tiny tots to dance.)* We want all the little ones to come out and dance.

(Sound: Drumming, jingling, all sounds fade.)

Scene Eleven

(MARGE's house. Music: Flute. Sound: Ambient interior sounds.)

MARGE: We should call Wanda Shewanda. See if she'll sell us another set.

LORRAINE: And if she can't?

SARAH: Be kinda hard to come up with a matching set.

GRACE: What will we tell her, Marge?

LORRAINE: We can't say that our friend, in a fit of grandeur, made a gift of them.

MARGE: We can say we lost them.

LORRAINE: That's more than the truth, Aunt Marge, and it makes us look careless.

SARAH: We can say what's on our mind. Wanda Shewanda probably be able to read it anyway.

LORRAINE: How do you figure that, Sarah?

SARAH: She's got an inkling about things. Puts me in mind of Handsome that way.

(Music: Flute plays 'Handsome' signature.)

He always knew a thing would happen before it did. She knew right away what was ailing me.

Made this here pouch that I got to wear for my pleurisy. Works pretty good, too.

GRACE: Ever see anything like that?

LORRAINE: You should put it in your museum. Okay, who wants to call.

GRACE: Let's flip for it.

SARAH: I'll call.

(Sound: Telephone is lifted and dialing begins.)

LORRAINE: Are you okay, Sarah?

SARAH: Nervous, is all. It's ringing. Hello. Hello! *(Louder.)* Hello! Is…Miss Shewanda there? Shewanda.

MARGE: *(Stage whisper.)* Wanda Shewanda!

SARAH: I feel light-headed.

(Sound: Rustle of movement, a footstep and the telephone is passed.)

LORRAINE: Sit down, Sarah. I'll talk to her. Hello. Hi, is this Wanda Shewanda? Okay, you remember the ladies who came up from Tyendinaga? Yeah, that's right, the beads. No, I'm the daughter. Grace is my mother. Yeah. The single one. Okay. *(Stage whisper.)* Ma, did you tell her I was looking for a husband?

GRACE: *(Underneath.)* Sarah mighta mentioned it.

LORRAINE: Yeah, I'm here. Wanda, it's about the beads. See, our friend, yeah, Kathleen! That's the one. Yeah, well, what she did was, well, she completely forgot that they were a prize and… *(Slight pause.)* Yeah! She did! To her daughter. Well, the prevailing opinion, here is that we should…ah, replace the beads and not say anything to the daughter, because, well… *(Slight pause.)* When do we need them?

MARGE: The draw is two weeks today but we got to know sooner.

LORRAINE: Wanda? Let us know as soon as you can. How much? A hundred dollars?

MARGE: A hundred dollars!

LORRAINE: Aunt Marge says that's fine. What's that? Keep them out of water? *(Pause)* Why's that? Do they melt? *(Pause.)* Okay, and thanks.

              (Sound: Phone hung up.)

MARGE: What'd she say?

LORRAINE: She can't promise. She'll call us.

MARGE: We'll have to sell more tickets to pay for the beads. Be kinda hard without a prize to show.

GRACE: Why don't we take a picture of May wearing the beads and cut off her head so nobody can recognize her?

LORRAINE: Oh, Ma.

SARAH: That'd set people to guessing who's neck was wearing the beads.

LORRAINE: You know, it'd be a lot easier to go to May and explain what's happened.

SARAH: *(Sudden sharp intake of breath.)* Ah.

GRACE: We can't interfere like that, Lorraine.

LORRAINE: But, Ma, it's the truth.

GRACE: Well…sometimes it's kinder to hold back the truth.

MARGE: You know, we might have to sell the tickets off the reserve.

SARAH: We could sell at the IGA, Marge.

GRACE: Lorraine? How about the Legion?

LORRAINE: Ma, why are you asking me?

GRACE: Maybe you can find a nice retired general to spend your reclining years with.

MARGE:	And we'll have to do the quilt for the undertaker's sister.
GRACE:	Quilt? In all this heat?
MARGE:	We won't sell enough tickets to pay Wanda Shewanda for another prize.
SARAH:	We still got to pay Isaac for making them cupboards. That's due in two weeks.
MARGE:	Kinda obliges us to make the quilt.
GRACE:	A quilt in two weeks, Marge?
LORRAINE:	That's your plan, Aunt Marge? The one with mercy in it?
MARGE:	It'll save Kathleen's feelings. Let her go on a while longer. She'd do the same for any one of us.
GRACE:	Kathleen can quilt like stink.
MARGE:	Grace, we can't ask Kathleen to quilt without telling her why.
GRACE:	Undercover mercy quilting! That's a new one. How we gonna hide from Kathleen for two whole weeks?
MARGE:	We can get rid of her.
SARAH:	Oh, my. You mean so we can inherit the beads?
MARGE:	You know these outings they got set up for the Elders? There's a purse factory and a hothouse. Well, I got tickets. Bought them with my birthday windfall.
SARAH:	I got one for that big jail up in Kingston.
MARGE:	Oh, that's the one I wanted.
GRACE:	Marge, you're so taken with jail. I don't know why.
SARAH:	It's them cops and robbers shows. You watch too many of them, Marge.
MARGE:	Let's give our tickets to Kathleen. She likes those

trips. We'll quilt while she's gone. Lorraine, you can try and sell some tickets. Describe the beads in your own words.

GRACE: Be a good way to make friends.

LORRAINE: It'll be a good way to lose them, too, Ma, if we don't come up with a prize.

MARGE: We can do it. And with the Creator's help—

GRACE: It's news to me if the Creator quilts.

Scene Twelve

(Local IGA Store. Sound: General background chatter, ringing of old cash registers.)

LORRAINE: Hi.

CASHIER: Sek:on!

LORRAINE: Sek:on! I'm Lorraine Brant.

CASHIER: You must be Grace's girl. The single one. You home for good now?

LORRAINE: Yeah. I'm helping to sell these tickets on a raffle.

CASHIER: I buy a ticket every year. I hear the prize is a necklace.

LORRAINE: That's right.

CASHIER: I'll take one. Say, you want to remind Sarah about her tobacco?

LORRAINE: Yeah. She's a little…busy.

CASHIER: It's these old people, eh? They forget.

Scene Thirteen

(The quilting bee at MARGE's. Sound: Rattle of tea-

cups, kettle whistle. Music: Flute begins and threads its way through scene.)

MARGE: Grace, take this tea in to Sarah. Don't spill it.

SARAH: It seems such a shame to cut up these shirts for the quilt, Grace. What would your husband say?

GRACE: Bull thought these shirts were the cat's whiskers. Made him look like he just walked away from a chain gang.

SARAH: They suit the quilt.

GRACE: Wonder what Bull'd think about the undertaker's sister wearing his shirts to bed.

SARAH: Don't know why you picked such a hard pattern, Marge, when we got so little time.

MARGE: We can't let the undertaker down.

GRACE: Marge, you're always going on about the undertaker. You must be taken with him.

MARGE: I want to stay on the good side of him, is all. He'll be the one to fix me up when I go. Maybe I'll get him to colour blue all round my eyes. Make me look like the chief's wife.

SARAH: I just want to look natural.

GRACE: You going to take your pipe with you, Sarah?

(All laugh.)

Scene Fourteen

(Legion Hall. Sound/Music: Ambient beer hall sounds, occasional voice calling, footsteps, chairs being moved. Country and western song, e.g. Hank Snow, playing.)

LORRAINE: Excuse me, folks, I've got raffle tickets in aid of the Elders' lodge.

EARL:	The Elders' eh? Old Davey's up there.

EARL: The Elders' eh? Old Davey's up there.

LORRAINE: That's right.

EARL: He's a vet, eh? Marches in all our parades. I'll take one.

LORRAINE: The prize is a necklace. Make a nice—

EARL: Ah, I never win anything. I always liked Davey, eh? Tell him Earl said hello.

LORRAINE: Thanks.

Scene Fifteen

(MARGE's house. Music: Flute threads through scene.)

SARAH: Marge, what d'you say we use this old dress for the binding?

GRACE: I know that dress.

SARAH: You gave it to me, Grace. Must be near twenty years ago.

GRACE: And now you want to turn it into a quilt for Miss Undertaker?

SARAH: Well, it's pretty near wore out.

MARGE: Use something else, Sarah.

SARAH: Grace, the dress you got on would look good in this quilt.

GRACE: I'm glad my corset don't match the quilt.

SARAH: It's too bad Kathleen's got to miss this.

GRACE: What's she missing? She's living the life of Reilly, visiting outhouses and what have you and we're working away so fast—

SARAH: I'll say. We got a quilt half done in a week. I never saw the likes of it.

MARGE: We're like them actors in a silent picture.

Scene Sixteen

(*Bowling alley. Sound: Bowling alley soundscape. Establish and continue under:*)

CARL: Hey! I know you. You're Grace's daughter.

LORRAINE: That's right.

CARL: I'm Carl.

LORRAINE: The undertaker?

CARL: Uh, huh. And you're the retired teacher.

LORRAINE: I'm a ticket seller today.

CARL: The beads. Very unusual beads, don't you think?

LORRAINE: They're rare. I've never seen…

(*Voice/Sound: Bowler makes a strike, followed by cheer.*)

LORRAINE: …anything like them. You got quite a crowd here.

CARL: Yeah, it's a good bunch.

LORRAINE: Think I could sell a few tickets?

CARL: Sure. They know Kathleen. She bowls. I thought she'd be here.

LORRAINE: She's on a trip…to a purse factory, I think.

CARL: She leads a charmed life.

(*LORRAINE laughs.*)

I thought maybe she just forgot. Listen. I'll sell the tickets for you and drop off the money later.

LORRAINE: Okay. Stay for coffee.

(*Sound/Biz: Another strike and cheer.*)

Scene Seventeen

> (*MARGE's kitchen. Music: Flute 'presence'.*
> *Sound: Kettle whistles.*)

MARGE: Who wants tea?

GRACE: I don't need tea. I need Geritol.

SARAH: I'll take tea. We got a fine looking quilt here, Marge.

MARGE: Twelve stitches to the inch and no shortcuts. I knew
            we could do it. We just got to believe in ourselves, is
            all.

GRACE: I'll believe when I see this quilt done.

MARGE: That's just eyesight, Grace.

SARAH: Marge is talking about faith, Grace. About seeing
            what can't be seen with the naked eye, like.

GRACE: Thought that was just seeing things!

> (*Sound: Yap of the tiny dog.*)

MARGE: Lorraine's coming.

> (*Sound: Yap and the engine shutting off.*)

SARAH: That dog's psychic.

> (*Sound: Door opens quickly and slams.*)

LORRAINE: Well! I sold another ten tickets! At the hospital!

GRACE: Ain't nobody asking to see the prize?

LORRAINE: Not yet, Ma. But, in two days, when we make the
            draw, the winner's gonna want to see the prize.
            Wanda Shewanda call?

MARGE: Not yet.

SARAH: Wanda Shewanda had a vision when she was
            making the beads.

GRACE: Was she seeing things?

LORRAINE: Go on, Sarah.

SARAH: Happened last spring, after a late snow fall. The water was swollen from the run-off. It was a nice day, she said, and it felt good to be outdoors. She looked down and saw a turtle just stopped by the stoop, like. She asked it where it had come from and went on to say, to commiserate, like, about the long winter just passed. Then it left and went into the water. Soon as it got in, the water turned real blue, just like the beads. She said the water looked just like one of them prizes on *The Price is Right*.

GRACE: Do you believe that?

LORRAINE: Don't you, Ma?

GRACE: Maybe I forgot how to believe. It must be fifty years since anyone on this reserve heard tell of a vision. If you owned up to one today, they'd lock you away. I blame it on them missionaries. We lost a lot on account of them.

MARGE: You don't lose anything unless you agree to let it go.

LORRAINE: Like the beads, Aunt Marge?

MARGE: That's different, Lorraine.

LORRAINE: There is a lot that we had and a lot we lost. Not because we agreed. We just didn't speak up!

MARGE: I mean the deep, down things that makes us who we are. We still have that.

LORRAINE: We could all learn something from Old Davey. He saw what we're losing and stood up and made a speech about it.

SARAH: Wanda Shewanda said we should keep them beads out of the water. *(Pause.)* You try on the beads, Grace?

GRACE: What are you driving at, Sarah?

SARAH: You put your best wig in the washer, by mistake, and… *(Pause.)*

MARGE: What else, Sarah?

SARAH: I tried them on. And that old crow that hangs around my yard relieved hisself in my rain barrel. Spoiled all that good water I was saving. Didn't you try them on, Marge?

MARGE: I did.

SARAH: Remember how you spilled the soup?

MARGE: I fell in it.

SARAH: All these accidents had something to do with water.

GRACE: Are you saying they're jinxed?

SARAH: I hope nothing happens to May.

MARGE: You must be tired after all that quilting, Sarah.

GRACE: It's that pipe. You must be inhaling.

SARAH: We should all get some rest.

MARGE: We'll get our rest bye and bye.

GRACE: You mean sleep, Marge, or rest?

MARGE: Both.

GRACE: I'd rather sleep now. Save the rest for later.

Scene Eighteen

              (LORRAINE's bedroom. Sound: Knock at the door, door opens.)

GRACE: Lorraine?

LORRAINE: What is it, Ma?

GRACE: Let me sleep with you tonight.

              (Sound: Door closes, bedsprings creak.)

LORRAINE: Sarah scared you, huh?

GRACE: Sarah's been scaring us all since we were girls. Tell me about the city.

LORRAINE: What do you want to know?

GRACE: Were the people nice?

LORRAINE: Some were.

GRACE: What about the white people?

LORRAINE: That's who I meant.

GRACE: Did you have friends there?

LORRAINE: Of course, I had friends, Ma.

GRACE: Any men friends, I mean?

LORRAINE: Some were men.

GRACE: White men?

LORRAINE: Yes. Aren't you sleepy?

GRACE: And you didn't meet one you wanted to marry?

LORRAINE: You wouldn't have wanted me to marry a white man, Ma.

GRACE: Well, only as a last resort. It's better with your own kind.

LORRAINE: I want to march to my own drum, Ma. Not somebody else's.

GRACE: You left it too long.

LORRAINE: No. I've always been that way. Maybe because I was the only one.

GRACE: I couldn't conceive of any more.

LORRAINE: One was enough, huh?

GRACE: I believe we raised you right.

LORRAINE: Of course you did.

GRACE: To be kind to others and not think only of yourself.

LORRAINE: Marriage is more than an act of kindness, Ma.

GRACE: It's a hundred acts of kindness every day, going back and forth, between husband and wife.

LORRAINE: What about love? Look at Sarah.

GRACE: Sarah's been sweet on Handsome since she was in pigtails. Still carrying the torch and the man's been gone nearly ten years. *(Pause.)* There's a lot of widowers on the reserve. *(Pause.)* Was it a white man?

LORRAINE: Who?

GRACE: The man who asked?

LORRAINE: There was no man.

GRACE: You said there was.

LORRAINE: I know. Because I think it disappoints you that I wasn't asked.

GRACE: I wasn't asked either.

LORRAINE: Go on!

GRACE: No. I saw that everybody around us was getting married so I said to your father:Bull, looks like we're the only single ones left. What d'you say we get hitched?

LORRAINE: What did he say?

GRACE: *(Mimicking BULL.)* Good idea.

LORRAINE: That's it? That's all he said?

GRACE: He wasn't big on words.

LORRAINE: Were you afraid of getting left behind?

GRACE: Seemed like such an awful thing for a young girl.

LORRAINE: You think it's awful for me?

GRACE: You got no one, and when I'm gone—

LORRAINE: Ma?

GRACE: Yeah?

LORRAINE: Don't be sorry for me.

GRACE: Is that why you said you were asked?

LORRAINE: In a way and I didn't want you to be sorry for you either, because I think you take it personally that I wasn't asked. *(Pause.)* Sometimes it's kinder to hold back the truth.

GRACE: You must have learned that in the city.

LORRAINE: I'm learning it from you.

Scene Nineteen

(MARGE's kitchen/phone. Music: Flute 'presence'. Ambient kitchen sounds, coffee perking.)

SARAH: Should be hearing from Wanda Shewanda any day now.

MARGE: The draw's tomorrow.

GRACE: The clock's running out.

LORRAINE: Maybe I should call her.

SARAH: Oh, she'll call. These things take time, Lorraine.

LORRAINE: We can't take what isn't there, Sarah.

                (Telephone rings.)

                I've got it.

                (Sound: Scrambling as phone is picked up.)

LORRAINE: Hello?

WANDA: *(Filtered voice throughout.)* Wanda Shewanda calling the ladies of Tyendinaga.

LORRAINE: Hello, Wanda.

WANDA: Who's this?

LORRAINE: It's Lorraine here.

WANDA: The single one?

LORRAINE: The one and only.

WANDA: I'm afraid I got bad news.

LORRAINE: Oh, no.

WANDA: See, the berries is pretty well all gone, eh. Just a few here and there that got left after the picking.

LORRAINE: Oh, yeah.

WANDA: Might have to wait till next year.

LORRAINE: What does that have to do with the beads, though?

WANDA: That's how I get the colour. See the berries got to be boiled down.

LORRAINE: You can't use frozen?

WANDA: No good. Plus you got to add a few things, you know, to set the colour. I could make red, maybe. My boy was out to Moose Jaw for a big Pow-Wow out there. Brought home a bushel of berries. They're red. I don't know what you call them.

LORRAINE: They must be Saskatoons.

WANDA: I could try using them.

LORRAINE: Just a minute, Wanda. (To others.) She can make red ones, Aunt Marge.

MARGE: No. They got to be blue.

LORRAINE: Wanda? You see, blue is what everybody saw when they bought the tickets.

WANDA: That's too bad. Ever try those berries?

LORRAINE: No.

WANDA: Might make good jam. How's Sarah?

LORRAINE: Sarah? She's fine.

WANDA: Too bad about them beads, eh? They look so old, like something the ancestors wore. Seem like they got old all by themselves. Could be on account of the turtle, though. A lotta power in that turtle. You got any water down there?

LORRAINE: We got the Bay of Quinte.

WANDA: I took something from the water when I made the beads. I shoulda give something back. Kinda bothers me.

(Sound: Receiver clicks and loud buzzing is heard.)

LORRAINE: Wanda? She's gone.

GRACE: Looks like we're sunk!

Scene Twenty

(Outdoors. Sound: The bustle of movement, screen door opens, the sound of water lapping against the shoreline fades up and continues throughout:)

LORRAINE: All those tickets sold on a prize we don't have. You know what that's called?

MARGE: Is it a scam?

LORRAINE: It's fraud, Aunt Marge. We could go to jail for it.

GRACE: You know what they do to you in jail? Make you wear clothes that look like Bull's shirts.

SARAH: Who's that down by the shore, Grace? Getting in the boat?

GRACE: Speak of the devil! It's May!

MARGE: Looks like she's going fishing.

SARAH: My, my.

(Sound: Hurried footsteps down the stairs.)

GRACE: Lorraine! Where you going?

LORRAINE: *(Calling back.)* To see May.

GRACE: Wait for me!

MARGE: No telling what she'll say. We better go down there.

             (Sound/Biz: Footsteps, somewhat slower, down the stairs, followed by some huffing and puffing.)

SARAH: Lorraine's got a mind of her own. Speaks it whenever she likes, too. She takes after you that way, Grace.

LORRAINE: *(Shouting as though equidistant between May and the others.)* May! Wait!

GRACE: Lorraine! Wait for us!

Scene Twenty-One

             (Water's edge. Sound: Water is lapping against shore. Boat oars are being paddled. Sound: Footsteps running along dock.)

LORRAINE: May! Wait! Where are you going?

MAY: Fishing. Want to come?

LORRAINE: Out in the water?

MAY: That's where they are, city slicker. I'll get you a fish. What kind you want?

             (Biz: Huffing and puffing is more present. The others have come to the shoreline.)

LORRAINE: *(Calling out.)* Get me a pickerel!

GRACE: I'll take a catfish! And get Sarah a trout!

MAY: *(Voice is if from a distance.)* You want me to smoke it for you, Sarah? *(Followed by laughter from shore.)*

MARGE: Was she wearing the beads?

LORRAINE: No. Let's go!

Scene Twenty-Two

> *(Doorway to MAY's house and inside. Sound/ Music: Door creaks open. Radio is playing in background, "Delilah" by Tom Jones.)*

LORRAINE: The door's open.

> *(Sound: Muffled footsteps as women enter.)*

GRACE: Who's that singing? Sounds like that guy always giving away his clothes.

> *(Sound: The radio volume is lowered. Music: Flute 'presence'.)*

LORRAINE: That's better. Okay. Let's look for the beads. Try not to move anything. What's the matter, Ma?

GRACE: We need a pie.

LORRAINE: No, we don't.

GRACE: Be better if we had a pie.

LORRAINE: Ma, we didn't break in. The door was open.

MARGE: Look what's here. The picture we had taken with our first quilt. Must be near forty years ago.

GRACE: Let me see.

MARGE: There's Kathleen and there's you, Grace. Remember your permanent wave? Look, Sarah, here you are.

SARAH: Something's wrong.

LORRAINE: What is it, Sarah? You should come away from the door, just in case—

> *(Sound: Rustle of feet.)*

SARAH: I don't see May.

GRACE: May wasn't born when we had this picture taken, was she, Marge?

SARAH: I don't see May out on the bay. She just disappeared, like. Swallowed up by the water.

LORRAINE: Don't say that, Sarah.

                (Sound: Muted turtle rattle.)

GRACE: Take a picture of this, will you? Our prize beads lying here on this old trunk!

MARGE: Let me see.

GRACE: Let's make a run for it. Here. You take the beads, Sarah.

SARAH: The turtle's gone.

                (Flute: Punctuates the idea. Sound: Car engine is heard faintly.)

LORRAINE: Somebody's coming. Geez, it's the police!

                (Sound/Biz: Mad scramble to hide, eager footsteps scurrying.)

GRACE: The jig's up!

LORRAINE: Just sit down.

                (Sound: Scramble to chairs.)

                Stay quiet. If he comes in, I'll say we're waiting for May to come with our fish.

                (Sound: Engine stops. Car door opens and closes. Footsteps on gravel, a knock on the door and the pounding of a heartbeat. There is a second knock, the heartbeat is louder.)

POLICEMAN: *(Muffled.)* Hey, May? *(Pause.)*

MARGE: Answer the door, Lorraine.

LORRAINE: Sssh. He's looking for May.

POLICEMAN: *(Muffled.)* May?

MARGE: You better answer the door.

                (Sound: Door opening.)

Scene Twenty-Three

> *(The front door of MAY's house. Sound: Exterior sound, a car passing on a gravel road, faint sound of water.)*

LORRAINE: Hi! You looking for May? She went fishing.

POLICEMAN: You're Grace's girl.

LORRAINE: That's right.

POLICEMAN: You visiting May?

LORRAINE: Just waiting for her. She's getting me a pickerel.

POLICEMAN: Give her these, will you? Say, are you the one selling the raffle tickets?

LORRAINE: Why?

POLICEMAN: The wife was telling me. Said you got some artist to make a necklace.

LORRAINE: That's right.

POLICEMAN: You got any left? The wife's birthday's coming up. I might get lucky and win it for her.

LORRAINE: I think so.

POLICEMAN: Can you come to the station?

LORRAINE: Now?

POLICEMAN: No. Not right away.

LORRAINE: Okay. I'll…give these to May.

POLICEMAN: Sure thing. You know, I was thinking… *(Pause.)*

> *(Sound: Heart pounding rises briefly during pause.)*

There's a guy at the station…he's…single, too. We kid him about it. Says he's waiting for the right one.

GRACE: *(Whispered.)* Who's he talking about?

POLICEMAN: Somebody in there with you?

LORRAINE: It's my mother. She's waiting for a catfish. I'll tell May you came by.

POLICEMAN: Okay.

(Sound: Door closing.)

Scene Twenty-Four

(Interior of MAY's house. Music: Flute 'presence'.)

GRACE: Let's make a run for it.

LORRAINE: We can't leave now. The police know we're here. We have to wait for May. And give her these.

MARGE: I s'pose we got to mind these minnows now.

LORRAINE: We have no choice.

SARAH: And no telling what's become of May. Look at them clouds.

(Sound: Loud roll of thunder and a crack of lightning.)

What'd I tell you?

GRACE: Well, why don't we make a pie while we're waiting.

MARGE: Grace, sit down. You're not yourself. Who's got the beads?

SARAH: I got part of them right here.

LORRAINE: Ah, geez, are they broken?

GRACE: What part do you have, Sarah?

SARAH: The part that goes round the neck. The turtle's gone.

MARGE: We got to put them back where we found them.

LORRAINE: Put them back?

(Sound: A loud crackle of lightning.)

MARGE: They're May's beads now, cause Kathleen give them to her.

LORRAINE: But they weren't Kathleen's to give.

MARGE: May don't know that.

LORRAINE: Ah, geez! Why didn't you say something before? Sarah? What do you think?

SARAH: Kathleen give May the beads for her birthday. She forgot where they came from. Forgetting is Kathleen's secret. Belongs to her. We got to keep it safe for her.

LORRAINE: You don't think May'd understand?

MARGE: It's not our place to ask.

LORRAINE: We're right back where we started. We don't have a prize.

MARGE: I s'pose we'll have to give back all the money we got for the tickets?

LORRAINE: You can't give back the money. What about the museum? And Sarah's wampum?

SARAH: We still got to pay Isaac for them cupboards.

LORRAINE: What about Wanda Shewanda's heart and soul, gone into a beautiful necklace that's…going back in time, that's going to be lying on some old trunk? You're going to sacrifice everything just so Kathleen can go on forgetting. I just don't get it.

MARGE: You've been away too long.

SARAH: It's not your fault, Lorraine. It's easy to forget.

GRACE: I blame it on the city.

LORRAINE: Look, this thing about Kathleen. It can't be that big a secret. Even the undertaker mentioned it.

GRACE: Oh? You met the undertaker?

MARGE: Lorraine's blushing.

GRACE: Let me see.

LORRAINE: No, Ma. Aunt Marge is making me blush. Cut it out now. We've got a pickle to think about.

Scene Twenty-Five

                (Inside. Sound: A thunder roar and crackle of lightning. Door swings open and footsteps clomp in.)

MAY: Somebody say pickerel?

LORRAINE: Holy cow! Is that a pickerel, May?

MAY: I suppose you thought it came in cans.

MARGE: That's a fine looking fish.

GRACE: Must be near ten pounds, wouldn't you say, Sarah?

SARAH: At least. May, you got a way with fish. Puts me in mind of Handsome.

                (Music: Flute plays 'Handsome' signature.)

                Never went out to fish that he didn't come back with a string of them.

MAY: What are you doing here? You should be up at the jail.

MARGE: What for?

MAY: That's where Ma is.

SARAH: What did she do?

MAY: Nothing, Sarah. She's up there watching a kung fu match.

MARGE: We only had one ticket.

GRACE: We flipped for it.

SARAH: Kathleen's gonna tell us all about it.

MAY: So…what are you doing here?

LORRAINE: Oh, you mean here? *(Pause.)* Well, I thought I'd wait for the pickerel…and while I was waiting I got to thinking about the beads.

MAY: What beads?

SARAH: Ooooh!

MAY: Sarah, are you alright?

SARAH: Just a little lightheaded is all.

GRACE: Must be that pipe. We should take you home right away.

MAY: No. Stay. And have some tea.

LORRAINE: You were wearing some beads at the IGA?

MAY: Yeah. You saw them, Sarah.

LORRAINE: Sarah said they were a lot like the prize.

SARAH: A little like them.

LORRAINE: We've been selling raffle tickets on a string of beads that are not unlike the ones you have.

MAY: I'm sorry. You lost me. Say that again.

LORRAINE: See, these beads that we had—

GRACE: Went all the way to Manitoulin Island to get them.

MAY: You say you had them?

LORRAINE: That's right.

MAY: What happened to them?

LORRAINE: Well…

MARGE: We lost them.

MAY: What does that have to do with beads I was wearing at the IGA?

LORRAINE: Well… Sarah just remarked on how—

SARAH: I was saying how little they looked like—

LORRAINE: No, Sarah, you said they looked a little like the ones
            we lost.

SARAH: Yes, a little, I s'pose they did kinda put me in mind
            of—

MAY: Ma gave them to me for my birthday. Jesus, Sarah,
            are you saying Ma gave me the beads you lost?
            That's stealing!

SARAH: It was an accident, like—

MAY: You mean she stole them by accident?

MARGE: No. Kathleen'd never do such a thing.

LORRAINE: Ma, tell May about the beads.

GRACE: We should flip for it.

SARAH: They fell in the bay! By accident, like. Ain't that
            right, Marge?

MARGE: Kinda looks like they're gone for good.

GRACE: We need one of them frogmen to get them. Like that
            one always wearing a toque falling backwards off
            his boat.

MAY: Ma didn't tell me you lost your prize.

SARAH: Cause she didn't know, that's why.

MARGE: We didn't want to tell her.

GRACE: She worries and…it gives her gas.

LORRAINE: May? We'd like to buy your beads.

MAY: Jesus, Lorraine! They were a gift! I can't sell them.

SARAH: You want to be careful with them.

MAY: I am.

SARAH: Especially round water.

MAY: I try to keep them dry. Is that what you mean,
            Sarah?

SARAH: Accidents happen. You had any accidents, May?

GRACE: Sarah, you gonna take us to the Twilight Zone again?

MAY: The other day at the IGA, the day I saw Sarah, I dropped a bottle of magnesia. It slipped right out of my hands. Jesus, it made an awful mess and you know that cat that hangs around?

MARGE: The one always napping on the shelves?

MAY: That's the one. It appeared out of nowhere and was lapping up the magnesia like it was clotted cream. Haven't seen it since.

SARAH: Funny how those things happen.

LORRAINE: Maybe we could make a trade, May?

MAY: *(Pause.)* What have you got?

LORRAINE: We got a quilt.

MAY: I could use a quilt. I don't know, Lorraine. It's still a little like selling.

GRACE: I traded Sarah a skip rope for a rag doll. Remember, Sarah?

SARAH: It was a doll my ma made.

GRACE: It was a good trade.

SARAH: Yeah. It was a good trade.

GRACE: Sarah learned to skip just like Jersey Joe Walcott.

LORRAINE: The quilt's blue and white. It'd look nice in your bedroom… I imagine.

MAY: A double?

LORRAINE: Yeah.

MAY: Blue and white sounds good.

MARGE: Twelve stitches to the inch and no short cuts.

GRACE: Got my late husband's shirts in it. May he rest in peace. My, but he loved those shirts.

MAY: If Ma knew I traded the beads she gave me and, knowing her, the way she is, she probably looked far and wide to find them...

MARGE: Yes, I'd say she'd did.

MAY: Well, if she found out, she'd be hurt.

LORRAINE: We won't say a word, May. I promise.

MAY: Can you keep a secret?

ALL: (Same time.) Yes.

MAY: Grace?

GRACE: Yes.

MAY: I don't like asking you to do something that's...against your nature.

SARAH: You got the beads handy, May?

MAY: Yeah, Sarah. They're right beside you on the trunk. I'm surprised you didn't see them there.

SARAH: Where's the turtle?

MAY: How'd you know about the turtle?

SARAH: When I first saw them, they had a turtle.

MAY: Yeah. Here it is. It fell off. I don't see how. Nothing looks broken.

              (Sound: Muted turtle rattle continues under:)

SARAH: Maybe it just wanted to be free. I got an idea in mind. Just come to me now.

LORRAINE: Does it have mercy in it, Sarah?

SARAH: It's fulla mercy. Come on outside. Keep watching while I take this turtle down to the bay.

              (Sound/Biz: Footsteps and then a door opening.

Scramble for the shoreline. Sound: Water grows louder.)

MAY: *(Calling.)* Hey, where you going? There's tea and Ma's rhubarb pie.

Scene Twenty-Six

(Outdoors. Sound: Water lapping against shore, very present. Exterior room tone plus a few birds. Muted turtle rattle continues under:)

MAY: What's she doing?

GRACE: What you got in mind, Sarah?

SARAH: A vision.

GRACE: Like Wanda Shewanda?

SARAH: *(Voice heard faintly.)* Maybe.

MAY: What's she doing?

MARGE: She's gonna set that turtle free. *(Calling.)* Careful on those rocks, Sarah. Mind your new hip.

(Sound: Muted turtle rattle fades, water lapping faintly. Sound: Footsteps on stones.)

MAY: Jesus! Look at the water!

LORRAINE: Ooooh!

MARGE: It's a vision.

GRACE: After all these years.

LORRAINE: I wonder what Handsome would make of that.

(Music: Flute plays 'Handsome' signature. Sound: Fade up water lapping against shoreline. Fade up the song from the Pow-Wow singers.)

The End.

MOURNING DOVE

EMIL SHER

Emil Sher was born and raised in Montreal. After teaching English in rural for Botwswana for two years, he returned to Montreal to pursue an M.A. in Creative Writing at Concordia University. He is the author of three plays for the stage, *Derailed* (nominated for four Dora awards in 1995); *Underwater, Overseas* and *Sanctuary*. His radio dramas include *Benefit of the Doubt* (*Stereodrama*); *Denial is a River* (*Morningside*); and *Hideous, Hideous* (*Sunday Showcase*). *Mourning Dove* was a finalist for the Grand Prize and Special Jury Prize at the 1996 International Radio Drama Festival in Moscow. It has also been broadcast in Australia. Sher has a number of screenplays in progress.

He lives in Toronto with his wife and his two young daughters, Sophie and Molly.

Mourning Dove was first broadcast on *Morningside*, on Tuesday, January 30, 1996, with the following cast.

DOUG RAMSAY	R.H. Thomson
SANDRA RAMSAY	Martha Burns
TINA RAMSAY	Annick Obansawin
KEITH MARTEL	David McFarlane
CORP. CRAIG PIERCE	Ken James
GORDON BELLAIR	Robert Parson
BARCLAY	Jonathon Welsh
CHISHOLM	Philip Akin
DR. KOVACS	Maggie Huculak
JUDGE	Lynn Deragon
ELDON	Wayne Ward
GWEN	Catherine Hayos
VERA	Kathryn Miller
ALBERT	Ross Manson

Producer	Gregory J. Sinclair
Production Assistant	Kate Nickerson
Recording Engineer	Janice Bayer
Sound Effects	Anton Szabo
Casting Director	Linda Grearson
Script Editor	Dave Carley

For My Father

Please note that all the courtroom scenes and testimony are from the transcripts of an actual trial, with some modifications.

Scene One

> *(Outside TINA RAMSAY's Bedroom. Sound: TINA's laboured breathing. Continues under:)*

SANDRA: *(Off.)* Doug. *(Beat.)* Doug. *(Approaching.)* Come to bed.

> *(Sound: TINA's breathing rises, then fades.)*

This has become a regular habit, you know, you standing there, watching her like some faithful dog. *(Pause.)* I can't remember the last time you came straight to bed.

> *(Sound: DOUG coughs.)*

Every night, the same detour. *(Pause.)* Standing there isn't going to change a thing. *(Pause.)* I'm going to bed. You coming?

> *(Sound: Faint breathing of DOUG and TINA.)*

Good night. *(Off.)* Good night.

> *(Sound: Off, SANDRA closes bedroom door. Sound: TINA moans. DOUG exhales.)*

Scene Two

> *(Courthouse steps. Sound/biz: Media frenzy as reporters swarm around DOUG, shoving and shouting. Continues under:)*

REPORTER 1: Mr. Ramsay, how will you plead?

REPORTER 2: Did you talk it over with your wife?

REPORTER 3: Was it a question of mercy?

(Sound: "Mercy" reverberates in a rapid succession of different inflections: a statement, a plea, a question, a sneer, and finally, a whisper.)

Scene Three

(Courtroom.)

COURT
CLERK: Douglas J. Ramsay, would you stand up please. Indictment: Douglas J. Ramsay (born 7th of June 1953) in the Province of Alberta stands charged that on or about the 21st day of November, A.D. 1994 in the Province of Alberta he did unlawfully cause the death of Tina Catherine Ramsay and thereby commit first degree murder—

KEITH: *(Off.)* No. He didn't do it. Not Dougie. No, no.

(Sound/biz: Mumbling and rumbling as court spectators react to outburst.)

Not Tina. Never, never.

JUDGE: Sit down or you will be escorted out of this courtroom. *(Beat.)* Continue.

CLERK: ...he did unlawfully cause the death of Tina Catherine Ramsay and thereby commit first degree murder contrary to Section 235 (1) of the Criminal Code. Douglas J. Ramsay, do you understand this charge that has been read to you, sir?

DOUG: Yes.

COURT
CLERK: How do you plead?

DOUG: Not guilty.

Scene Four

(Medical examination room. Sound: TINA crying out in pain as she lies on table. Continues under:)

SANDRA: Okay, Tina, that's a girl. Dr. Kovacs is almost done.
                 Almost.

DR. KOVACS: Her left hip has a nice range. The right hip concerns
                 me.

DOUG: She never lies down on her right side.

DR. KOVACS: You can see how the skin on the left side is starting
                 to break down.

SANDRA: She favours that side. You know. It's more
                 comfortable.

DR. KOVACS: I want to try and move her right hip. I'll need your
                 help.

SANDRA: Daddy and I are going to turn you over, sweetheart.
                 Okay?

DR. KOVACS: On the count of three. One. Two. Three.

                 *(Sound/biz: TINA cries in pain as her body is
                 shifted. SANDRA whispers words of comfort.)*

                 Her right hip has no range. It's too—

DOUG: It's too painful.

                 (Sound: A sharp cry from TINA.)

DR. KOVACS: *(Beat.)* Yes.

Scene Five

                 *(Doctor's office. Sound: Off. A baby crying in
                 waiting room. Sound: Off. Phone ringing.)*

RECEPTIONIST: *(Off; into phone.)* Dr. Kovacs' office.

                 *(Sound: Door closing, muffles waiting room
                 sounds.)*

DR. KOVACS: Tina is going to need another operation.

                 *(A discomforting silence as the news sinks in. We
                 can hear, faintly, the infant crying in the waiting
                 room.)*

SANDRA: I remember what you did to her back. All those rods and wires. I don't want you drilling any more holes in my baby.

DR. KOVACS: I understand that, Mrs. Ramsay. But you've seen what Tina's hip is doing to her. The pain it's causing.

DOUG: What about drugs? You know. Instead.

DR. KOVACS: I don't think so. We would have to use fairly powerful drugs. If they're taken with the medication she's using to control her seizures there could be some serious side effects. It could be even harder for her to swallow. Food could end up in her lungs. She could get very sick.

SANDRA: No more. *(Beat.)* No more.

DR. KOVACS: Tina's in too much pain to do nothing. Her hip is too far gone.

DOUG: What does that mean? Too far gone.

DR. KOVACS: We have to do what we call a salvage procedure.

SANDRA: Salvage?

DR. KOVACS: Try and picture the ball at the top of Tina's thigh bone, and the hip socket it fits into. There's something called "articular cartilage", a tissue which allows this ball and socket to move freely. The trouble is, Tina's ball has been sitting out of its socket for too long. The ball is damaged and has lost its shape. The cartilage has worn away. We can't put the ball back into the socket.

SANDRA: Why not?

DR. KOVACS: It would be like putting an arthritic hip back together again. It's doomed to continue to be painful.

DOUG: How are you going to do this salvage business?

DR. KOVACS: In simple terms, I have to take away the damaged part and cover the end of the bone with muscles, and hope—

DOUG: What do you mean, "take away"?

DR. KOVACS: Remove.

DOUG: You saw it off, don't you? You're gonna saw off the ball part.

DR. KOVACS: *(Pause.)* The ball part and about the top quarter of the thigh bone.

> *(Sound: SANDRA reacts.)*

> The surgery is necessary. We have no alternative.

DOUG: That's not the end of it, is it? Half the kids with palsy, they don't make it to their tenth birthday. You told us that. You showed us that study.

DR. KOVACS: Fifty percent survived past age ten. Tina is twelve.

DOUG: No more operations?

DR. KOVACS: The chances of Tina's other hip dislocating is a real possibility. And because of her weight loss, I expect there may have to be more intervention.

DOUG: Intervention.

DR. KOVACS: A feeding tube…

> *(Sound: A bereft SANDRA reacts.)*

> Or another method of giving her nutrition that would bypass the mouth and swallowing mechanism. But let's not jump too far ahead. We have to schedule Tina's hip surgery. The sooner, the better. I have an opening in three weeks. Let's do it then.

Scene Six

> *(Flashback: RAMSAYS' home. The hallway. Sound: TINA's laboured breathing. Continues under:)*

SANDRA: *(Off.)* Doug. *(Approaching.)* Doug. Come to bed. *(Pause.)* We've got to get up early tomorrow. I don't

want to be late for church. *(Beat.)* You look tired.
You look terrible. You shouldn't have gone into the
store today. Not after what the doctor told us
yesterday. You should've taken the day off. You
should get some sleep.

(Sound: TINA's breathing.)

I'm going to bed. Good night. *(Off.)* Good night.

*(Sound: TINA's breathing continues, cross-fades
with a ticking clock in RAMSAYS' bedroom, which
continues under:)*

Scene Seven

*(RAMSAYS' bedroom. Sound/biz: DOUG
climbing into bed, SANDRA being roused.)*

SANDRA: *(Groggy.)* I didn't think you were ever coming to
bed. What time is it?

DOUG: What's the colour of pain?

SANDRA: What?

DOUG: Pain. You think it has a colour?

SANDRA: *(Fully awake.)* What are you talking about?

DOUG: Today, at the store. Keith comes up to me, he's all
upset. A customer had come up to him and said he
needed some paint for his pane. What colour would
Keith suggest?

SANDRA: A window pane.

DOUG: You know how Keith can scramble words. Like
when he carved Tina the mourning dove.

KEITH: *(Reverb.)* To wake her up in the morning.

SANDRA: What'd you tell him about the colour of pain?

DOUG: I told him what the customer meant. But I've been
thinking about it ever since. If Tina's pain had a

	colour, what colour do you think it would be?
SANDRA:	Red pain. Blue pain. What does it matter? Pain is pain.
DOUG:	A colour might make things easier.
SANDRA:	For who?

(An uncomfortable pause.)

I don't think Tina can take much more.

(Another pause.)

| DOUG: | Today I picked up a 40-pound bag of gravel. You know what went through my mind? This bag of gravel weighs more than my daughter. |
| SANDRA: | Some nights, I wish she would just go to sleep and not wake up. |

(An unearthly silence as both SANDRA and DOUG absorb SANDRA's statement.)

Scene Eight

(Flashback: RAMSAYS' kitchen. Sound: Bacon frying, kitchen sounds.)

SANDRA:	You going to church dressed like that?
DOUG:	I'm going into work.
SANDRA:	Can't it wait?
DOUG:	I asked Gwen to look after Tina till I got back.
SANDRA:	I thought we should both be there. Make our prayers twice as loud.
DOUG:	I'll take a raincheck.
SANDRA:	Why're you opening up on a Sunday anyhow?
DOUG:	I didn't say I was opening up. I have work to do.

SANDRA: Even God rested on the seventh day.

DOUG: God didn't own a hardware store.

SANDRA: I thought if we both went. I don't know. Maybe things would turn out all right.

DOUG: I've said my prayers.

SANDRA: You want me to pick you up at the store, then? On the way back from church?

DOUG: I'll meet you back here.

Scene Nine

(Flashback: RAMSAY's hardware store, back room. Sound: Electric sander. The sander becomes louder as DOUG approaches and enters.)

DOUG: *(Over sound of sander.)* Keith. *(Beat.)* Keith.

            (KEITH shuts off sander.)

KEITH: I didn't hear you come in.

DOUG: How could you, with that thing going a mile a minute. What are you doing here on a Sunday morning? Store's closed. You should be home.

KEITH: I want to finish this. For Tina. My sander wasn't working. I let myself in. Is that okay?

DOUG: I wasn't expecting you.

KEITH: It's a birdhouse. See?

DOUG: How long do you plan on being here?

KEITH: I have to finish sanding the roof.

DOUG: I got some work to do.

KEITH: You think she'll like it?

DOUG: I'm sure she will.

KEITH: You'll have to put in near her window. So she can look out and watch the birds.

DOUG: I'll be out front if you need me.

KEITH: You think they'll like it?

DOUG: What?

KEITH: The birds. You think they'll like the house?

DOUG: For sure. *(Beat.)* I have to get some work done.

KEITH: For sure.

        (Sound: KEITH turns on sander. Fades.)

Scene Ten

        (Flashback: RAMSAY's hardware store.)

KEITH: Is it okay if—

DOUG: Christ, you scared me.

KEITH: I didn't want to bother you. You looked real busy. Like you were talking to someone who wasn't there.

DOUG: How long have you been standing there?

KEITH: Couple of minutes.

        (Uncomfortable silence.)

    Is it okay if I take a couple of sheets of sandpaper?

DOUG: Help yourself to whatever you need.

KEITH: What's the hose for?

DOUG: What do you mean, what's it for?

KEITH: I was just asking.

DOUG: What does someone use a hose for?

KEITH: For watering.

DOUG: Well, that's what it's for. It's for watering.

Scene Eleven

(*Flashback: RAMSAYS' home.*)

CHISOLM: (*Reverb/Courtroom.*) Most importantly, you will also hear evidence on how Douglas Ramsay, on November 21st, once Sandra had gone to church with the kids, set about going to his hardware store, getting some pieces in terms of fittings and pipes together, getting some rags, putting them in the truck, then driving back home...

(*Sound: Hockey game play-by-play on the television. Sound: DOUG closes door behind him as he walks into house.*)

DOUG: Gwen?

(*Sound: The game gets louder as DOUG approaches living room.*)

A hockey game at this hour?

GWEN: Last night's game. I taped it.

DOUG: What's the point of watching when you already know the score?

GWEN: I don't know. I kinda like knowing how things'll turn out before they begin.

DOUG: Tina enjoying?

GWEN: I don't know. Not like before. She. She doesn't react like she used to.

DOUG: Maybe the game's getting too fast for her.

GWEN: Maybe. (*Beat.*) You want me to stay and help prepare lunch?

DOUG: We're all right.

GWEN: You sure? I don't mind.

DOUG: I'm sure.

GWEN: Okay, then.

                 (Sound: GWEN puts on coat.)

                 Bye, Tina. Bye, Mr. Ramsay.

                 (Sound: GWEN walks away. The game continues.)

                 Mr. Ramsay?

                 (Sound: More hockey noise. DOUG is lost in thought.)

                 Mr. Ramsay?

                 (DOUG still doesn't react.)

                 (More forcefully.) Mr. Ramsay.

DOUG: *(Startled.)* I...I didn't.

GWEN: I forgot my tape.

DOUG: *(Lost.)* The tape.

                 (Sound: The hockey crowd is silenced when TV is clicked off; video tape is ejected from VCR.)

GWEN: Bye.

                 (Sound: Front door is closed.)

DOUG: Tina, sweetheart. It's time to go.

                 (Sound/biz: DOUG picks up TINA and carries her in his arms.)

CHISHOLM: *(Reverb/Courtroom.)* ...driving with Tina in the truck out to the shed where she was then propped up with the rags while he rigged an apparatus up to run from the exhaust and through the sliding window of the cab and started the vehicle and then eventually shut the vehicle off and returned Tina to her bed in the house and there awaited the return of Sandra and the children.

Scene Twelve

(*Courtroom.*)

PIERCE: I told him I wanted him to listen very carefully because this was a serious matter. I started by saying that we are not here to judge him. I understand the situation you are in and we empathize with you. We have no choice but to do the job we have to but at the same time we'll assist him in getting through this situation as best we can. "We have spoken to several people. Everyone said the same thing, that you are a caring person, a good person. At the same time, we know that this was not a natural death. Your daughter was in a great deal of pain. Doug, after considering all that is known, I have no doubt that you caused your daughter's death." There was no response from him and I noticed that his eyes were glassy with tears. I continued, "This is not something that you wanted or planned to do. You loved your daughter very much." At that point he nodded yes. "This is something that you felt you had to do out of love for your daughter, isn't it, Doug?" There was no reply. "I can imagine this is very difficult for you and I feel bad." I repeated that he was a loving father and I said, "You only did what you felt was best for her out of love for your daughter." Again there was no reply and I repeated it. I asked, "Isn't that right, Doug?" At that point he was close to crying. I said again, "That's what happened, isn't it, Doug? Isn't that right?" He replied, "My priority was to put her out of her pain." I asked, "That's what you thought was right, wasn't it?" and he began nodding his head yes. At this point there were tears flowing freely.

Scene Thirteen

(*Flashback: RAMSAYS' front steps. Sound: (Off.) Car engine is turned off; car door slammed shut.*)

DOUG: How was church?

SANDRA: *(Approaching.)* We'll have to wait and see.

DOUG: What does that mean?

SANDRA: Why aren't you wearing your jacket?

DOUG: Didn't notice.

SANDRA: You step out and figure it was still summer?

DOUG: Didn't give it much thought.

SANDRA: Where's Tina?

DOUG: Sleeping.

SANDRA: At this time of day?

DOUG: What time is it?

SANDRA: One-thirty. When did she fall asleep?

DOUG: About an hour ago.

SANDRA: She okay?

DOUG: What do you mean?

SANDRA: How was she when she fell asleep?

DOUG: *(Pause.)* Peaceful.

SANDRA: Well, I hate to disturb the peace, but I gotta wake her up.

DOUG: Now?

SANDRA: She's gotta eat.

DOUG: I'm not hungry.

SANDRA: Are you okay?

Scene Fourteen

(Courtroom.)

PIERCE: I asked him if he wanted to tell me how he did it. He says he drove the truck to the shed with her in it, hooked up a hose to the exhaust and ran it into the cab. I asked, "How long was she in there for?" and he replied, but I don't recall what he said for a time and I asked, "And she just fell asleep?" He said, "Yes, she just fell asleep," and then he added, "If she'd have started to cry I would have taken her out of there," and then again he himself began to cry. *(Pause.)* I said, "Doug, you have told us briefly what happened. I would like you to start at the very beginning and go through exactly what took place. Go slow. I'll put it to paper." He started, "She's been in pain for years. Ever since she was born she's had trouble." He hesitated. I said, "Go on."

(PIERCE's voice cross-fades with DOUG RAMSAY's.)

"She had an operation a year ago in August to straighten her back, put rods in."

DOUG: Prior to that her hip was dislocated intermittent so they operated on her back. They knew there would be one on her hip but the hip was secondary, didn't seem that serious. Then since May or June almost full time dislocated. Each time you moved her there was pain so the operation for the hip was planned for this time of year. It was more complicated than what we had expected so we just couldn't see another operation. She'd be confined to a cast for I don't know what the time was so I felt the best thing for her was that she be put out of her pain.

Scene Fifteen

(Flashback: RAMSAYS' house. Sound: Anxious knocking on front door. There is no reply. Anxious knocking resumes. More silence, until…)

DOUG: *(From behind door.)* Who is it?

KEITH: Me.

(Sound: DOUG opens door. Sound: (Off.)

SANDRA's muffled, animal-like crying. Continues under:)

I just finished it. What do you think?

DOUG: Very nice.

KEITH: I painted the roof red. They like bright colours—

DOUG: Maybe.

           (Sound: SANDRA's crying intensifies, can be heard more clearly.)

KEITH: Is that Tina?

DOUG: *(Pause.)* No.

KEITH: Can I show it to her?

DOUG: *(Lost in thought.)* What?

KEITH: The birdhouse. Can I show it to Tina?

DOUG: When?

KEITH: I'll show it to her. Then we can put it up near her window.

DOUG: No.

KEITH: You don't like it?

DOUG: Not now.

KEITH: I can make another one.

DOUG: Now is not a good time.

KEITH: When's a good time?

DOUG: Leave it here for now.

KEITH: Tina won't see it down there.

DOUG: Leave it here. *(Beat.)* Please.

Scene Sixteen

(Coffee shop. Sound/biz: Clatter of cutlery, small talk in booths. GORDON BELLAIR approaches CPL. PIERCE's booth, sets down his coffee.)

GORDON: Craig, you gotta minute?

PIERCE: You know what the service is like around here, Gordon. I got at least fifteen. What's on your mind?

GORDON: Keith.

PIERCE: Keith made a nuisance of himself in court today.

GORDON: I heard.

PIERCE: He didn't want to hear what I had to say about Doug. About what Doug had told me he'd done. He kept crying out, saying it wasn't true. The judge warned him twice, then threw him out of the courtroom.

GORDON: I know. He dropped by my place this afternoon.

PIERCE: That's not front page news, Gordon. He spends half his life at your lumberyard, the other half at Doug's store.

GORDON: He didn't stick around. Usually he sticks around. You know. Collecting scraps of wood and whatnot. Today he was all funny like. Real nervous. Just stood around with his hands in his pockets. Then kinda disappeared.

PIERCE: Is there a moral to this story?

GORDON: I drove by Keith's apartment. To make sure he was alright. Mrs. Sanderson, she told me he never showed up for supper.

PIERCE: Keith's not one to miss a meal.

GORDON: He could be in danger. He could be. He doesn't... You know what Keith is like.

PIERCE: I don't have a crystal ball.

GORDON: My rifle's gone, too. The one I keep in the office.

PIERCE: Rifle?

           (The higher stakes suddenly spark PIERCE's interest.)

GORDON: I'm worried.

PIERCE: I'll look into it.

GORDON: I was wondering.

PIERCE: What were you wondering, Gordon?

GORDON: I was thinking maybe there was... I don't know. Some kind of connection.

PIERCE: What kind of connection?

GORDON: He was awfully attached to the girl. Always making her gifts out of wood. Maybe what happened to Tina set him off. Scared him. *(Beat.)* You know. They were both... *(Pause.)*

PIERCE: Both?

GORDON: *(A considered pause.)* They were both different.

Scene Seventeen

           (Courtroom.)

JUDGE: Good morning. It is your job to decide the facts from the evidence you have heard, then to apply the law to those facts, and, having done that, to try and reach a verdict as to the guilt or otherwise of Douglas Ramsay. You cannot let your passions or your feelings stand in the way of your reason. The questions you must ask here are whether you are satisfied beyond a reasonable doubt that Douglas Ramsay did in fact cause the death of his daughter and, if so, did he do so intentionally. It is convenient here to deal with Mr. Barclay's argument. He says Tina's death should be characterized as a suicide, that all her life her parents were required to make her choices for her, and that they had a moral and legal obligation to make the proper choices— choices that were in her best interest, that she was entitled to commit suicide and that her legal guardians were authorized to make that choice for her because she was incapable of making it herself. I must tell you as a matter of law that this argument is untenable. Mr. Chisholm says that this was a calculated, coldblooded murder motivated by self-interest. The evidence did not leave that image in my mind and I doubt that most people would see it that way. Mr. Barclay says that if Mr. Ramsay did intentionally cause the death of his daughter by some means of unlawful act, then it was a compassionate act of kindness. That seems to be more likely. Each of you will have your own view but both characterizations beg the question which is, did Tina's father intentionally cause her death by means of some unlawful act, namely by putting her in the cab of the truck and polluting it with exhaust and, if so, was it planned and deliberate? First degree murder is one that is planned and deliberate. Murder that is not first degree is second degree murder. There are only three possible verdicts here: guilty as charged, not guilty as charged but guilty of second degree murder, or not guilty.

Scene Eighteen

(Courthouse steps. Sound/Biz: A refrain of the melee that greeted DOUG on the first day of the trial: a media frenzy as REPORTERS swarm around DOUG RAMSAY, shoving and shouting.)

REPORTER 1: How do you feel?

REPORTER 2: Did you want to speak in your own defence?

REPORTER 3: Do you think the jury believes you're innocent?

(Sound: "Innocent" reverberates in a rapid

*succession of different inflections: a statement, a
plea, a question, a sneer, and finally, a whisper.)*

Scene Nineteen

*(Holding cell. Sound: The clank-and-grind of a
metal jail door being closed and locked.)*

SANDRA: What d'you think's going to happen?

DOUG: Don't know.

SANDRA: You might end up going to jail.

DOUG: I might.

SANDRA: For a long time.

DOUG: I know.

SANDRA: Jail is for criminals. You're not a criminal.

DOUG: No.

SANDRA: Are you scared?

DOUG: *(Pause.)* No.

SANDRA: I am.

DOUG: I'll be all right.

SANDRA: You know how sometimes you wish for something.
Then it happens. Then you wonder if it would've
happened if you hadn't wished so hard.

DOUG: You don't think I should've done it.

SANDRA: I didn't say that.

DOUG: What're you saying?

SANDRA: I feel guilty.

DOUG: I'm the one on trial.

SANDRA: We've been through this together.

DOUG: Always.

SANDRA: From the start. You and me.

DOUG: And her.

SANDRA: And her.

DOUG: I miss her.

SANDRA: It's been hard.

DOUG: What would you have done?

SANDRA: I don't know.

DOUG: What was I supposed to do?

SANDRA: You did what was best for her.

DOUG: *(Pause.)* That's right.

SANDRA: No one understands.

DOUG: No. They don't. *(Beat.)* Sometimes I don't.

SANDRA: They don't know what it's like.

DOUG: I don't understand. Not always. Sometimes I don't understand any of this. *(Beat.)* Do you?

SANDRA: Not always. Not yet.

DOUG: Green.

SANDRA: Green?

DOUG: The colour of pain.

SANDRA: They found him, you know. Keith. Sitting on top of the fire tower. He won't budge.

DOUG: It's a green colour, the pain. An old green.

SANDRA: Her pain doesn't have a colour any more.

DOUG: I'm talking about me.

SANDRA: She loves you, still.

DOUG: *(Pause.)* You think?

Scene Twenty

>   *(Coffee shop. Sound/biz: Clatter of cutlery, small*
>   *talk in booths.)*

ALBERT: Vultures.

VERA: Who?

ALBERT: Those TV people.

ELEANOR: Today's judgement day. They hand down the
                  verdict. That's why they're hovering like flies.

ALBERT: They've been swarming all week, trying to make
                  something out of nothing.

ELDON: C'mon, now. Tina wasn't "nothing".

ALBERT: Did I say that? That's not what I said.

VERA: Yes it is.

ALBERT: It's not what I meant.

ELDON: What did you mean?

ELEANOR: He means Doug Ramsay is a good man and doesn't
                  deserve all this…all this…

VERA: Attention.

ELEANOR: Thank you.

ALBERT: The press people, they love this kind of thing. This
                  circus. They never knew Tina.

ELEANOR: And they don't know Doug. They'd know he
                  wouldn't. They'd know he wasn't guilty.

ELDON: He admitted he was. Told Craig Pierce right to his
                  face.

ALBERT: Just 'cause he did it doesn't mean he's guilty.

VERA: Then what does "guilty" mean?

ALBERT: I don't know the law. I know Doug. He did the right thing. He did what was best.

ELDON: Best for who?

ALBERT: Whose side are you on?

ELEANOR: He's playing devil's advocate.

ALBERT: The devil doesn't need an advocate. He's got those press people working for him full-time.

VERA: They're just doing their job.

ALBERT: If they'd stayed away this whole thing would've blown over real quick. They turned this town into a coast-to-coast courtroom. The whole country's one big jury.

ELEANOR: I half-expect to see Keith on television any day now. I'm surprised they haven't done a story about him yet.

ALBERT: Keith isn't news. Keith is slow.

VERA: He's been up on that tower all week, like some frightened bird. That's news.

ELDON: What's he afraid of?

VERA: Maybe he wants to set a record or something.

ALBERT: Don't waste your time trying to understand Keith. Keith is Keith. Doug's the one on trial. He's the one who's innocent. *(Beat.)* No one understands that. No one cares.

ELEANOR: He used to feed Tina by hand. Like a baby.

SANDRA: *(Testimony/reverb.)* Her food all had to be blended with no lumps in it.

ELEANOR: Poor thing couldn't so much as hold a spoon.

ELDON: How does a devoted father turn around and do what he did?

ALBERT: You playing devil's advocate again?

ELDON:	I'm thinking out loud.
VERA:	He loved her.
ALBERT:	Like nothing else.
ELDON:	I know he loved her.
ALBERT:	Since when does being a loving father make you a criminal?
ELEANOR:	People do funny things 'cause of love.

Scene Twenty-One

> *(Courthouse steps. Sound/biz: A quick refrain of the melee that greeted DOUG on the first day of the trial: a media frenzy as reporters swarm around DOUG, shoving and shouting.)*

REPORTER 1:   Was justice done?

> *(Sound: The word "justice" reverberates in a rapid succession of different inflections: A statement, a plea, a question, a sneer, and finally, a whisper.)*

Scene Twenty-Two

> *(CPL. PIERCE's patrol car. SOUND/BIZ: The media swarm, quickly muffled as… Sound: Car door is slammed. Sound: Engine is revved. Car drives off.)*

PIERCE: I guess you won't be missing them anytime soon.

DOUG: *(Pause.)* No.

PIERCE: I guess they're just doing their job.

> *(He waits for DOUG to respond. DOUG remains silent.)*

> Listen. Before I take you to… I know I shouldn't be doing this, but…I…I know it's wrong. You know

Keith has had a bad reaction to all this. I guess you
know that. Do you know about the rifle? *(Pause.)*
Maybe you don't. He had a rifle with him when he
first went up the tower. Took a couple of shots at
me. *(Nervous laughter.)* He doesn't have the gun
anymore. Swapped it for food. You know what
Keith's appetite is like. He won't come down. He…
I was thinking you should have a talk with him.
You're the only one. Maybe now that the trial is
over he'll listen to you. You get along real well.
What d'you think? I can't force you or anything. I
mean, I shouldn't even be… I thought it's something you'd want to do. *(Beat.)* Do you?

Scene Twenty-Three

*(Fire tower. Sound: Birds circling above tower.
Strong wind. Continues under DOUG's grunts as
he climbs up last rungs of tower. He steps onto
platform.)*

KEITH: You?…

*(Sound: DOUG collapses on platform, exhausted
from climb.)*

You're here.

DOUG: *(Catching breath.)* Me. You getting enough to eat?

KEITH: I knew you didn't do it.

DOUG: It's cold up here.

KEITH: You loved her too much.

DOUG: That sleeping bag enough?

KEITH: I knew you'd come up here.

DOUG: What's that?

KEITH: What does it look like?

DOUG: A horse.

KEITH: For Tina. I carved it myself. Tina loves horses.

DOUG: You shouldn't have done that.

KEITH: You don't like it?

DOUG: You shouldn't have carved right into the railing like that.

KEITH: They can fix it. They can put in new wood. From Gordie's lumberyard. *(Beat.)* You want a biscuit?

DOUG: I'm not hungry.

KEITH: Some juice.

DOUG: I can't stay.

KEITH: Too cold for you?

DOUG: No.

KEITH: Remember that time I built a fire up here?

DOUG: Keith, you can't stay up here, either.

KEITH: *(Laughing.)* A fire on a fire tower.

DOUG: They're waiting for us down below.

KEITH: I wasn't scared.

DOUG: I promised Cpl. Pierce we'd come down together.

KEITH: Tell him to go away.

DOUG: I can't do that.

KEITH: Tell him this is my tower.

DOUG: When we get down, he'll take you home.

KEITH: Tell him to leave us alone.

DOUG: He has a job to do.

KEITH: You'll drive me home.

DOUG: I can't do that.

KEITH: *(Peers over tower.)* Where's your truck?

DOUG: They're taking me away, Keith.

KEITH: Away?

DOUG: Prison.

KEITH: *(Pause.)* No, no.

DOUG: Yes.

KEITH: No, no, no, no.

DOUG: Yes.

KEITH: You didn't do it.

DOUG: That's not how they saw it.

KEITH: Who?

DOUG: The jury. They announced the verdict this morning.

KEITH: Tina. Tina, Tina. Tinatinatina.

DOUG: She's not in pain. Not anymore.

Scene Twenty-Four

(Court, flashback.)

BARCLAY: How much involvement did Douglas have in Tina's day-to-day care?

SANDRA: Lots. When he was home I never had to lift her. He would lift her. When she got home I would give her a drink and then he would lift her from her wheelchair to the couch or wherever she had to go. He did all the bathing. Especially the last year of her life. I was pregnant and I couldn't lift her so he'd bath her. I bathed her once in October but I think the rest of the time that year he did all the bathing. If she threw up, he would—he would clean her up. He would bath her. He changed her diapers, wet or dirty. He was—he was just there for her.

(Pause.)

(Testimony/reverb.) Her muscles were very, very tight and it was starting to twist her body, twist it very badly. They cut a lot of muscles, like her toes, her heel chords, the outside of her knees, abductor muscles. They put her in a body cast so that her back—it was to try and keep these muscles, like from not tightening up, like to try and keep them loose.

Scene Twenty-Five

(Fire tower. Sound: A strong, menacing wind.)

KEITH: She's dead.

DOUG: She went to sleep and she never woke up.

KEITH: She—she wasn't a dog.

DOUG: No, she wasn't.

KEITH: She was your daughter.

DOUG: She still is.

KEITH: She was my friend.

DOUG: I know.

KEITH: You killed her like she was a dog. It's what you do to dogs. You put them to sleep.

CHISHOLM: *(Reverb/Courtroom.)* It is not open season on the disabled.

DOUG: She died peacefully.

KEITH: How do you know? How do you know how she was feeling? *(Beat.)* How do you know?

DOUG: I held her in my arms.

KEITH: Did you ask her?

DOUG: Ask her what?

KEITH: If she wanted to die.

DOUG: She couldn't speak. You know that.

KEITH: She could laugh.

SANDRA: *(Testimony/reverb.)* She liked to watch bonfires. She liked to see things that moved. Like, if we were in the car and the windshield wipers were going, that would make her laugh when she was well, like when she was younger.

KEITH: She laughed when I gave her the mourning dove. Remember? Remember?

          (Sound: Wind fades.)

DOUG: *(Reverb.)* Tina, there's someone here to see you. Keith. You know Keith.

KEITH: *(Reverb.)* This is for you. For your birthday. A mourning dove. To wake you up in the morning. See? *(Beat.)* She smiled. She's smiling at me. *(Beat.)* If you move the dove up and down, you can pretend it's flying. See?

          (Sound: Reverb of TINA's laughter.)

          (Reverb.) She's laughing. She likes it. She's laughing.

          (Sound: TINA's laughter cross-fades with wind blowing across fire tower.)

DOUG: She used to laugh. When she was younger.

Scene Twenty-Six

          (Court, flashback.)

CHISHOLM: We submit that the Accused is guilty beyond any reasonable doubt of the first degree murder of his daughter. Now, while Tina may have been frail medically, she was fit enough for surgery and indeed there was an impending surgery coming. Before I go further, I just want to read to you one from the 12 Commandments for Parents of Children with Disabilities and it's just the first commandment. "Thou art thy child's best and most consistent advocate." I certainly suggest that is not what happened here. When we speak about Tina Ramsay, I'm sure the first thoughts that run through everyone's mind is that she was indeed very frail, a 38-pound, 12-year-old girl, couldn't walk, couldn't talk, who was totally dependent on everybody for all that she needed in life, and Sandra Ramsay certainly stressed that in fact Tina had seizures every day of her life. Almost everyone involved in this case seems to portray or suggest that Tina's was a very dreadful existence but I suggest that's simply not so. As Sandra said, Tina liked to sit outside. She liked to watch a fire, and which one of us doesn't like to sit there and watch a fire and think all kinds of thoughts. She would laugh at windshield wipers on the car. She would smile whenever she saw other members of her family because she recognized them all. She could laugh, she could smile, she could cry. What more, for her, did there need to be? Her care was no different than what you would give to one of your babies and indeed, it's no worse, just different. As Sandra put it, Tina was like a two or three-month-old baby and I suggest to you that your decision should be no different here in this case than it would be if the Accused had murdered a baby. Why should it be any different?

Scene Twenty-Seven

(Fire tower. Sound: Strong wind.)

KEITH: Maybe she wanted to live.

DOUG: They were going to operate again. Cut off part of a bone. But the pain wouldn't've stopped. That's no way to live.

KEITH: How do you know what she wanted? You're not God.

DOUG: I'm her father.

KEITH: Not the same.

DOUG: If she'd cried in the truck, I would've taken her out.

KEITH: God decides when it's time.

DOUG: She never cried.

KEITH: God's will.

DOUG: I would never hurt her.

KEITH: My granny says that all the time. God's will.

DOUG: Your granny didn't have seizures. Seizures, seizures, all day long.

KEITH: God's will.

DOUG: Stainless steel rods in her back.

KEITH: I know someone with a steel plate in his head.

DOUG: He isn't Tina. Tina is Tina.

KEITH: Tina is dead.

DOUG: Tina never had a chance. Not a fair one.

SANDRA: *(Testimony/reverb.)* When she was little I cried myself to sleep every night for a year. That's when I grieved. I did all my grieving when she was little. We lost her then.

KEITH: What you did wasn't fair.

DOUG: Don't tell me about fair and unfair. I lived with unfair every day of her life.

Scene Twenty-Eight

(Court, flashback.)

BARCLAY: All of the medical personnel emphasized that Tina's parents were in the best position to try and interpret what was going on in Tina's body and in her mind. They were in the best position to assess the pain that she was in and in fact throughout Tina's life Douglas and Sandra Ramsay made every single decision that was ever made by Tina. They decided whether she would eat, what she would eat, how much she would eat. They decided whether she would roll over, whether she would sit up, whether she would have a clean diaper, whether or not—even whether or not she would have a bowel movement. I suggest no one was in a better position than Doug and Sandra Ramsay to understand what kind of pain their daughter was in and even those who didn't know Tina perceived her to be in excruciating pain.

Scene Twenty-Nine

(Fire tower.)

KEITH: I'm not going down.

DOUG: You can't stay here.

KEITH: I like it here. Safe. *(Beat.)* Safe.

DOUG: It's safer down there.

KEITH: Not for me.

DOUG: Why not?

KEITH: Not for people like me.

DOUG: What are you afraid of?

            (KEITH doesn't reply.)

            What are you afraid of?

KEITH: *(Pause.)* You.

DOUG: Me?

KEITH: You.

DOUG: Why me?

KEITH: *(Pause.)* Are you going to kill me, too?

DOUG: *(Emotionally winded.)* What?

KEITH: Like you killed Tina.

DOUG: I would never hurt you.

KEITH: You killed Tina. We're the same.

DOUG: You're not the same.

KEITH: Same, same.

DOUG: Not true.

KEITH: Same because we're different.

DOUG: Tina had severe cerebral palsy. You—

KEITH: I've got Down's.

DOUG: You can't compare. It's two different— You don't understand.

KEITH: You don't understand.

DOUG: Tina was my daughter. You're my friend.

KEITH: A freak.

DOUG: You're not a freak.

KEITH: Some people say so. A freak of nature. Like Tina.

DOUG: You're not Tina.

KEITH: You killed her because she was different.

DOUG: Because of the pain.

KEITH: Pain made her different. If she had no pain, she wouldn't be different. You wouldn't have killed her.

DOUG: She was suffering.

KEITH: You don't kill something because it's different. It's not right. That's what my granny says.

DOUG: I wasn't thinking of you when...

KEITH: When you killed Tina. *(Beat.)* When are you going to kill me?

DOUG: I'm not going to kill you.

KEITH: How do I know?

DOUG: Keith...

KEITH: How do I know?

DOUG: I'm not like that.

KEITH: Tina didn't know you were going to kill her.

DOUG: She couldn't understand.

KEITH: She couldn't protect herself.

(DOUG steps forward.)

Stay away.

DOUG: I'm not going to hurt you.

KEITH: Don't touch me.

DOUG: We can climb down the tower together.

KEITH: I'm staying. I'm safe.

DOUG: You're safe down there.

KEITH: Stand back.

(Sound/biz: DOUG steps forward to comfort KEITH. KEITH misinterprets the gesture. They struggle briefly. KEITH begins to cry.)

Don't kill me. Please don't kill me.

Scene Thirty

(Courtroom. Duelling lawyers, flashback.)

BARCLAY: I urge you, when you look at this case, to look at it and say, what is the right thing to do in this case?

CHISHOLM: What gives Douglas Ramsay the right to wipe out potentially the next 30 years of Tina's life?

BARCLAY: If my client has committed a sin against God, God will judge him.

CHISHOLM: This is but one man's abhorrent decision because he no longer valued Tina's life as he did that of his other children.

BARCLAY: The only thing we're here to deal with today is whether or not the highest legal sanction known to Canadian law should apply to Douglas Ramsay. Should he be categorized as a first degree murderer?

CHISHOLM: I can only state that this was a murder most foul, callous, cold, calculating, heartless and not motivated by anything other than making his own life easier.

BARCLAY: I don't wish any of you to get the idea that in any way this trial is anything more than the trial of the guilt or innocence of Douglas Ramsay.

CHISHOLM: So the question arises, what is or what was Douglas Ramsay's cause, and I use that phrase because in an interview he said he wasn't taking up anyone else's cause, so what was his cause?

BARCLAY: This is not a cause. This isn't going to start some slippery slope argument that you need be worried about.

CHISHOLM: Are we saying that those who wish or care for us can determine our fate?

BARCLAY: Nothing about this case per se legalizes euthanasia.

CHISHOLM: Does the philosophy become, "Since we brought you into this world we can decide when you leave this world"?

BARCLAY: You only have to deal with this set of facts.

CHISHOLM: I would simply ask you just to remember and look at photo 32 in Exhibit P-1 of Tina. Think of her. Just for a moment.

BARCLAY: You only have to deal with what's the right thing in this set of facts.

CHISHOLM: She had presence.

BARCLAY: We only need to be concerned here about the justice of this case and whether or not your conscience would feel right in sending this man away with a conviction for first degree murder.

CHISHOLM: She had the right to live.

Scene Thirty-One

(Fire tower.)

KEITH: *(Crying; frightened.)* I don't want to die.

DOUG: I don't want you to die.

KEITH: Don't do to me what you did to Tina.

DOUG: No.

KEITH: Just because I'm different.

DOUG: No.

KEITH: I'm scared.

DOUG: I'm holding you.

KEITH: Don't hurt me.

DOUG: Never.

KEITH: You hurt her.

DOUG: I didn't see it like that.

KEITH: You hurt me.

DOUG: I see that now.

KEITH: *(Cries.)* Tina. Tinatinatina. *(Wipes his nose, sniffles.)* Why're you crying?

Scene Thirty-Two

(Courtroom, Flashback.)

JUDGE: There is no joy in this for anyone. I know you believe you did the right thing and many people will agree with it; however, the criminal law is unremitting when it comes to the taking of human life for whatever reason. Life was not kind to Tina but it was a life that was hers to make of what she could. I am left with no option but to order that you be sentenced to imprisonment for life without eligibility for parole until you have served ten years of the sentence. Mr. Ramsay, is there anything you want to say?

DOUG: I still feel I did what was right.

JUDGE: Yes, anything else?

DOUG: Well, my wife mentioned that it's not a crime to cut her leg off, not a crime to stick a feeding tube in her stomach, not a crime to let her lay there in pain for another 20 years. I don't think—I don't think you people are being human.

Scene Thirty-Three

(Fire tower.)

PIERCE: *(Off; from below tower.)* Doug? *(Beat.)* Doug, what's happening up there?

DOUG: We're coming down.

KEITH: What about the horse?

DOUG: Horse?

KEITH: The horse I carved for Tina.

DOUG: Let's leave it here. She would've liked it up here.

KEITH: She loved watching fires.

DOUG: *(Pause.)* She did.

KEITH: You wanna go down first?

DOUG: You go. I'll follow.

                    (The End.)

STOP TALKING LIKE THAT

JUDITH THOMPSON

One of Canada's best known and most celebrated playwrights, **Judith Thompson** has forged her career in a number of mediums, including radio television, film and stage. For CBC Radio Performance she has written a number of dramas, including *Sugar Cane*, *The Quickening*, *A Kissing Way*, *Tornado* (winner of the Nellie Award for best drama) and *White Sand*, which won the B'Nai B'rith Human Rights Award. Her stage plays include *Lion in the Streets* (winner of the 1991 Chalmers Award); *I Am Yours* (winner of the Chalmers and Governor General's Award); *White Biting Dog* (winner of the Governor General's Award) and *Crackwalker*. The latter was her first play, premiering in 1980 at Theatre Passe Muraille, and it continues to receive productions around the world, including London, England's Gate Theatre, Hudson's Guild Theatre in New York, and the Riverine Theatre in Wagga Wagga, Australia. Thompson's new drama, *Sled*, premieres at the Tarragon Theatre in early 1997.

Thompson's many television and film credits include *Life With Billy* and three works in development: *Les Biches*, *Upstairs in the Crazy House* and *Teenage Girls Save the Earth*. She has directed, acted and is a graduate of Queen's University (BA in drama and English) and the National Theatre School's acting program. Thompson lives in Toronto with her husband and four children.

Stop Talking Like That was first broadcast on *Monday Night Playhouse*, on April 24, 1995, with the following cast:

CATHERINE and SONJA .... Amber-Lea Weston

TRISH... Rachel Hethorn

MARY .... Nicole Parker

DRIVER and CDN. ANNOUNCER .... John Robinson

FERGUS .... Chris Wiggins

PAT .... Fay Maddison

ARTHUR .... Hardee Lineham

JOANNE .... Cyndy Preston

LIL .... Marion Bennett

MAILMAN (TONY).. John Bayliss

COP .... Damon Redfern

PILOT and AUS. ANNOUNCER...................... Brian Pearcy

TRACKER .... Rod Gidgup

Producer .... David Britton

Associate Producer......................... Sandra Jeffries-Broitman

Recording Engineer .... John McCarthy

Sound Effects .... John Stewart

Executive Producer .... James Roy

Casting Director .... Linda Grearson

Script Editor .... Dave Carley

Dedicated to my grandfather,
The Rt. Hon. Francis Michael Ford

Scene One

(Inside bathroom. JOANNE is in the bathroom. LILY and PAT are outside. Music: Percussion— haunting, aboriginal. Sound: Water running. Sound: LILY pounds on the door.)

LILY: Joanne, would you please get out of the bathroom, it's a quarter to nine! I don't want to be late!

JOANNE: Be out in a minute!

LILY: No! Now! This second. I don't want to have to get another late slip because you spend an hour weighing yourself.

(Sound: Pounding continues.)

JOANNE: *(Int.)* Okay, okay Joanne, we'll try once again: if the scales say you're over 77 pounds this time again, nothing for you to eat today, nothing.

LILY: Mum! Joanne won't get out of the bathroom again.

(Sound: LILY pounds on the door.)

PAT: Joanne, honey, please.

(Sound: JOANNE gets on the scales.)

JOANNE: *(Int.)* 78 pounds. You glutton. Nothing for you to eat for three days. Just water. Just water.

(Sound: LILY's frantic pounding continues.)

LILY: Joanne, it's five to nine!

(Sound: JOANNE opens the door.)

JOANNE: Sorry. It's my period.

LILY: Joanne, you're an anorexic. You haven't had a
                 period in a year.

Scene Two

                 *(School cafeteria. Sound: Talking, laughing of high
                 school kids.)*

SONJA: Martin's bringing a case of 2-4, and Sanders says he
                 can get some really good hash—

LILY: Oh my God Sanders is so hot.

SONJA: My folks go, "Now just a small party, Sonja, just
                 five or six close friends. We'll be calling from
                 Florida."

MARY: Meanwhile every kid in school is coming.

LILY: Except Insect.

SONJA: I still can't believe she's your sister, Lil. She is so
                 weird.

MARY: Look how she's lookin' at us. What does she want?

SONJA: I just can't believe you guys are sisters.

LILY: I can't either. She's always been a freak.

SONJA: Poor Lil. I would die if I had a sister like that.

MARY: Even the other freaks don't hang out with her.

LILY: She's always been by herself. Ever since she was
                 born.

Scene Three

                 *(Dining room. Family having dinner. Sound:
                 Cutlery, amplified chewing. P.O.V. JOANNE, and
                 the drone of the radio.)*

ANNOUNCER: That's forty below with the wind chill factor in old Thunder Bay. Remember folks, exposed skin freezes in three minutes.

(Sound: LILY turns off the radio.)

LILY: Forty below. Christ I'll be glad to get out of this country. I wish we could go tomorrow!

ARTHUR: Darling, please don't take the Lord's name in vain.

JOANNE: The cold isn't so bad, really. If you dress for it.

LILY: Joanne, you're such a freak.

PAT: Lillian, you are not to talk to your sister like that.

JOANNE: It's okay. I am a freak.

ARTHUR: Joanne, don't put yourself down. You offend God when you put yourself down.

JOANNE: I'm the only girl in grade ten who hasn't been invited to Sonja Mills' party Friday night. I must be a freak.

PAT: Are you going, Lil?

LILY: Yeah.

PAT: Why? Why would you go where they don't want your sister?

ARTHUR: I'm sure there's some reasonable explanation. Lil, why do you think they didn't invite Joanne? Reasonably.

LILY: Because, Daddy, look at her! She's a skeleton. And she always says weird things. Everybody laughs at her, and if Sonja invited her, nobody would come.

PAT: You little bitch.

ARTHUR: Patricia!

LILY: I'm sorry, ma mère, but it's true. She should know the truth. Look at her, she hasn't touched her food. Again.

JOANNE: I have so, I've stuffed myself.

LILY: Mum and Dad! Listen to her, she's crazy. She should be put in a hospital. You're crazy.

PAT: If you don't stop Lily, I'll sock you so hard you'll have to be put in hospital. Darling, won't you eat just a few veggies at least?

JOANNE: I did, Mum. Really. I'm stuffed.

LILY: She's gonna starve herself to death and you guys just stand by.

ARTHUR: Lillian. I have every faith that the Lord will not let Joanne starve to death.

LILY: Oh blind faith really helps, Dad.

PAT: It's a very complex issue, Lillian.

LILY: I'm finished, may I be excused?

JOANNE: I was thinking of writing a note to Sonja, just maybe, I don't know, asking her to give me a chance.

LILY: Joanne. She doesn't want you there. Don't make a fool of yourself.

JOANNE: But why? What have I done wrong? I'm a nice person.

LILY: You're different, that's all. They don't like anyone who's different. May I be excused?

PAT: No. Since we're all going to Australia next week, I'd like to play the travel game, you know, the one we used to play when you girls were little.

LILY: I'm out of here.

            (Sound: LILY gets up, pushing out her chair.)

PAT: Sit down, Lillian. You're part of the family. Lillian. Sit down. Thank you. When I think about Australia, I think about…sweat pouring down the back of my legs and the smell of burning wood. Jo?

JOANNE: You mean just things I've heard? Like, myths?

PAT: Anything.

JOANNE: An island.

ARTHUR: Settled by convicts. That's one of the first things I
             learned about the place. I remember thinking,
             "Wow, everyone there is related to a bad guy."

LILY: Hot surfer guys with all this blond hair on a white
             beach. With big hard-ons.

PAT: If you're trying to shock us you're failing.

JOANNE: Sharks. Very white, in a feeding—

LILY: —frenzy. Like the guys'll be, all over me. Ha ha.

PAT: I'm thinking of passionfruit. Daddy has a
             passionfruit vine in the backyard, they are the most
             delicious thing you have ever tasted. Honestly,
             unlike anything else.

ARTHUR: Eucalyptus trees. With those cute koala bears all
             over them, eating up the leaves.

PAT: Lamington Squares. Did I ever tell you about them?
             They're a kind of national cake with chocolate and
             coconut and gooey in the middle. Daddy and I used
             to make them all the time when I was a kid.

ARTHUR: "Kookaburro sits in the old gum tree, merry, merry
             king of the bush is heeee." I learned that at St. Pat's,
             grade two.

PAT: Jack Wallop, the aboriginal man who used to work
             on our land, he used to smile at me—and then one
             day he walked away.

LILY: This big famous rock, where people go camping?
             And this weird lady, she had her baby there and it
             just disappeared? And everybody thought she
             killed it, but she said it was the dingo.

PAT: Ayers Rock. I used to go there, with Daddy and
             Mum, camping.

(Music: Drumming melds into aboriginal drumming.)

JOANNE: Her baby disappeared?

LILY: Yeah, like she'd left it sleeping in the tent? And she's partying or whatever and she goes to check in and it's gone. All they ever found was like a pink sweater about a year later, under the dirt.

JOANNE: What's a dingo?

LILY: A wild dog.

JOANNE: A wild dog devoured the baby?

PAT: They don't know. People wore T-shirts saying, "The dingo is innocent." But they still don't really know.

JOANNE: Didn't three schoolgirls disappear there at the turn of the century?

ARTHUR: That was Hanging Rock.

(Sound: A distinctive sound indicating JOANNE's destiny—the sound will be repeated every time she or FERGUS gets a sense of this destiny. The sound should have an ancient, tribal, land-connected feel to it. It will be referred to as the "Destiny Sound" from now on.)

JOANNE: And they disappeared?

LILY: What's with Australia and rocks?

(Sound: "Destiny Sound".)

PAT: They started to climb while the others were napping, and...they vanished.

JOANNE: I wish.

PAT: You don't mean that, Joanne.

LILY: Nothing was found, not a fingernail, not a hair.

PAT: Maybe it was the dream time.

JOANNE:	Dream time?
PAT:	Yes, it's a…aboriginal sort of thing.
JOANNE:	The baby and the girls, they walked into the dream time.
ARTHUR:	You're looking a little pale, sweetie. Why don't you drink up your milk. *(Pause.)* Joanne, I asked you to please drink up your milk. Joanne! *Will you drink up your milk!*
JOANNE:	It is so dark in here all of a sudden. Does anybody else find it dark?
PAT:	I think maybe you'd better lie down, Joanne. I'll bring you some chicken soup later.
JOANNE:	Like right before all the light drains away.
PAT:	Jo, you're dizzy from not eating. Trust me.
JOANNE:	I haven't eaten in two years. This is different.
LILY:	*(Leaving.)* Why was I cursed with such a weird sister? I'm outa here.

(Sound: Door slams.)

PAT:	I guess we're all cursed.
JOANNE:	I know I am.

(Sound: "Destiny Sound".)

Scene Four

(Outside. Sound: Kookaburro in full sound, plus other birds. The sound should die down as the dialogue continues.)

FERGUS:	G'day Tony. Any love letters for me today, then?
MAILMAN:	See for yourself, Fergus.
FERGUS:	Nobody's interested in an old man, Tony.

MAILMAN: I know what you mean, Ferg. My old mum, she had the watery eyes, for about five years before she died. I just thought it was a condition, like, of the eyes, but I realized later it was, well, just what you say. The lack of interest.

FERGUS: You lose your self-confidence in yourself, if you know what I mean. In your body, first off, because it's bloody falling apart, and then yourself.

MAILMAN: In China they respect old age, I've heard, look up to it. The wisdom and that. That's the way it should be, I reckon.

FERGUS: I don't know, Tony. When I had an old dog on the— I took it out and I shot it.

MAILMAN: Oh come now, Ferg, if you was shot dead who would I have to talk to on my route?

FERGUS: Oh I'm just pulling your leg, Tony, you should know that. I'm not one to cry in me beer.

MAILMAN: Say, isn't your girl coming soon, with the family?

FERGUS: This time next week.

MAILMAN: Too bad the missus weren't alive to see them.

FERGUS: Ohh, it broke Maura's heart, her only livin' overseas. Not to see her grandchildren.

MAILMAN: Oh yes, I can see it would.

FERGUS: You know, I was thinking, strictly between yourself and me, I have a good life insurance policy, over a million. All for Patty of course. I should do her a big favour while she's here and go on a walkabout. Just… You know, disappear. They could use the money.

MAILMAN: You wouldn't get past the golf links, Ferg, with that leg.

FERGUS: Maybe I'll go back with them, to Thunder Bay, and sit myself on an ice floe, like one of them Eskimos. That'd be a way to go.

MAILMAN: I seen on telly, the polar bears, up there, they'll wander into the towns and grab up the little ones.

FERGUS: Way up in the north, maybe. Once every ten years or so.

MAILMAN: And snow covers the ground from late September well into June.

FERGUS: Some places, yes.

MAILMAN: And people freeze to death on highways, if their car breaks down.

FERGUS: Tony, all these stories, them's just myth, just rubbish. Them's not what a place is.

MAILMAN: What? What is what a place is, then Fergus?

FERGUS: I reckon it's…the quiet.

MAILMAN: Like in the bush, when all ya hear are the crows, like?

FERGUS: Like the dead. Layin' under the ground. From all the years.

MAILMAN: Get off it, Ferg, it's the smell. Any place ya go, there's a smell hits you. It's the type of food you eat, mixed with the body odour, and, the plants, I reckon. And every place has its own.

FERGUS: The dead speak to us in the quiet.

MAILMAN: Think so?

FERGUS: It's dark so sudden. Think my pressure's up.

MAILMAN: Do you want to sit down?

FERGUS: It's the daughter I'm troubled about. The eldest.

MAILMAN: Trouble is she? Into the drugs?

FERGUS: No no, that's the other one, but Joanne… I've been having these dreams.

MAILMAN: What kinda dreams?

FERGUS: Raw meat. She's eating the red raw meat. I've heard
                 the black fellas say raw meat means death. D'ya
                 reckon?

MAILMAN: I reckon you undercooked your evening chops.

                 (Sound: "Destiny Sound".)

                 I've never seen it so dark, quite so early. Have you?

Scene Five

                 *(Inside airplane. Sound: 747 taking off. The family
                 talks under the announcements.)*

PILOT: *(Speaks with Australian accent.)* Good evening, and
                 welcome aboard Quantas flight 309. This is your
                 pilot, James Naughton, speaking. My co-pilot is
                 Andrew Park, and we'll be flying at 10,000 feet
                 today.

JOANNE: *(Breathes fast, shallow breaths.)*

PILOT: Our first stop will be beautiful Honolulu,
                 approximate flying time, eight hours. The stewards
                 will be serving you a hot dinner at 21 hundred
                 hours, with your choice of beverage.

PAT: Joanne, are you alright?

JOANNE: *(Hoarse, breathless whisper.)* Yuh. Fine. Fine.

PILOT: The temperature in Honolulu is a balmy 87 degrees
                 Fahrenheit, so don't forget your sunscreen. It's a
                 dark and stormy night out there in Toronto so I do
                 advise you to keep your seatbelts buckled up. It
                 may be a bit of a rough ride, but we'll give it a go!
                 Enjoy your flight, ladies and gentlemen.

                 *(JOANNE's breathing has a terrified edge. The
                 following dialogue is under the above speech.)*

PAT: Just try to breathe deeply and calmly, sweetheart.
                 You're breathing too fast. Joanne? Joanne look at
                 me.

JOANNE: *(Her breathing continues.)*

PAT: Joanne? Arthur, there's something wrong with Joanne.

ARTHUR: Nonsense, she's fine, it's just good old fear of flying. This is a very safe airplane, honey. You have a much greater chance of being hit by lightning than crashing in this plane. Besides, Father Hanley back in Thunder Bay is saying a special mass for us, Joanne.

> *(Sound: The wings going down. Sound: "Destiny Sound".)*

JOANNE: *(Breathes fast.)*

PAT: Joanne. Sweetheart? Arthur, what's wrong with her?

ARTHUR: Joanne. Honey, look at me. Joanne.

JOANNE: I can't breathe very well. Dad? Remember when Aunt Janet died in that car accident?

ARTHUR: What the heck does Jan have to do with—

JOANNE: Did she know? Before? Like did she say anything at all to you, about dreams, or…

ARTHUR: Joanne. God does not plan the death of His children. He gives us free will. And sometimes things happen. But nothing, nothing is going to happen to you. Besides, Aunty Jan, may she rest in peace, had four double scotches in her, and she had no business driving a car.

> *(Sound: "Destiny Sound". JOANNE: Teeth chattering.)*

PAT: Joanne, you're shivering, dear. Are you cold?

LILY: Oh gimme a break. She's just putting on a show. Can't you guys see that?

JOANNE: I am not, Lily. I just… I'm having fear of flying, that's all. Even Wayne Gretsky has it, there's nothing freakish about it. *(Getting up.)* I gotta puke.

PAT: Joanne? Honey? Would you like me to come with you?

JOANNE: *(Leaving.)* No, Mum.

PAT: Are you sure? I could just stand outside.

JOANNE: *(Off.)* No thanks, Mummy.

LILY: Anorexics die of that, Mum, we learned it in health class. They die from their heart. What's her name, that singer, Karen Carpenter, 'member? "Close to you..." She died like that.

PAT: I know, Lily. Don't you think I'm worried sick about it?

ARTHUR: The next step is forcing her into a hospital, feeding her through tubes, and tying her to the bed. It's pretty drastic, Lillian.

LILY: I'm gonna go see if she's okay.

Scene Six

(Inside plane's toilet. Sound: JOANNE flushes toilet, as LILY knocks.)

LILY: *(From outside.)* Joanne, it's me. Can I come in?

JOANNE: Just a sec.

(Sound: JOANNE opens the door. Plane background up, then down as door closed.)

I'm just leaving.

LILY: Stay for a minute. I need to talk to you.

JOANNE: I really don't feel like being picked on or patronized right now, Lily.

LILY: I just want to talk to you. Joanne. Listen. I just wanted to say...just well, Sonja's party was pretty bad. I mean you didn't miss much.

JOANNE: I didn't want to *go* to Sonja's patty, Lil, I just wanted to be invited.

LILY: Basically it was just a grope, you know.

JOANNE: It's okay, Lil.

LILY: And I was thinking, you know, you are different, from the other kids at school, and I know that's hard, but if you go away to University or whatever, you'll find…well …people like you. Who think the way you do. You know? So…you shouldn't give up.

JOANNE: Why are you being so nice? Are you feeling okay?

LILY: I feel awful, actually. I'm nauseated, and my nipples are sensitive and my period is two months late.

                (Sound: LILY unzips her jeans and checks her underwear, then zips up, as:)

JOANNE: You had unprotected sex?

LILY: Serge won't use a condom.

JOANNE: Oh Lily.

                (Sound: LILY pulls out a cigarette.)

                Lily, you can't smoke in here.

LILY: Watch me.

                (Sound/Biz: She lights a match, JOANNE blows it out.)

JOANNE: You could cause an inferno in this thing, Lily. That's how Stan Rogers died, Lily, because somebody was smoking in the airplane toilet.

LILY: Who's Stan Rogers?

JOANNE: The Canadian folk singer? That Dad listens to all the time? You know, "May the Mary Ellen Carter rise again, rise again…rise again…" He died because he was saving other people, pushing them out before himself. He died because somebody had to have a smoke.

LILY: Okay, okay.

JOANNE: I wonder if he knew, when he stepped on the plane.

LILY: I wonder if this baby knows?

JOANNE: Is that what you're planning? An abortion?

LILY: I'm sixteen, Joanne, I'm not gonna have a baby.

JOANNE: But I wonder where they go? You know? All the…

LILY: Don't talk. Just don't talk.

Scene Seven

                       (Inside plane. The final descent. Sound: Plane landing.)

PILOT: Well it's a sunny 39 degrees Celsius in Adelaide today, so peel off the cardigans, and on with the sunhats. I hope you've enjoyed flying Quantas…please keep your seatbelts on while we taxi down the runway…

LILY: 39? Fantastic.

JOANNE: Daddy? The day that you said we miss cause of flying across the dateline.

ARTHUR: Thursday.

PAT: Thursday completely disappears. Gone.

LILY: Cool.

JOANNE: But where is it?

PAT: Good question.

JOANNE: Really, Dad. Where is it?

ARTHUR: Well, Joanne, it's just a—

LILY: Dad doesn't know.

PAT: It's a time zone thing, that's all.

JOANNE: But is the day inside us? Or did it just disappear?

LILY: Joey, you are so weird.

PAT: Lily, shut up.

PILOT: *(Slightly distorted.)* Please leave your seatbelts fastened while we taxi down the…

PAT: Oh Joanne, you're shaking again. Darling, I'm sure it's your blood sugar.

                 (Sound: "Destiny Sound".)

JOANNE: It's just so very dark.

PAT: It's not really, hon'. Oh Joey, my firstborn, what are you scared of?

JOANNE: Australia.

PAT: Listen. Remember your grandpa has an aviary in the shed with 300 tropical birds. And there's the passionfruit out back. You're going to be very happy. I know it.

JOANNE: I'm going to be happy?

PAT: Yes.

JOANNE: Will I be able to eat? Will I be able to eat again?

PAT: Oh God, darling, we hope so. We hope so.

Scene Eight

                 (The terminal. Note: PAT's normally Canadian accent subtly begins shifting to an Australian accent. Sound: Airport background.)

FERGUS: Hullo! Hullo! Patty!! Give your old dad a great big hug.

PAT: Oh Daddy, it is so good to see you!!

FERGUS: My Patty pat. Let me see you. Just as lovely as ever. And Arthur. How are you?

ARTHUR: Great to see you, Mr. O'Reilly. You're looking well.

FERGUS: I'm eighty-two and not a damn thing wrong with
              me! And will you look at the two of you. My lovely
              grandchildren Lillian, and Joanne. Oh, Joanne.

              (Sound: "Destiny Sound". Didgeridoo.)

JOANNE: Hi.

PAT: Are you alright, Dad? Do you want to sit down?

FERGUS: Fine, fine. I just...when I seen Joanne, I had one of
              them...what do you call them, like you've
              already...been through it?

JOANNE: Deja vu?

FERGUS: That's it, dear. Near knocked me over.

JOANNE: Me too. Seriously.

ARTHUR: Well, I'm sure it's all the excitement, I always get
              those things when I'm overexcited. It's the Lord's
              way of saying, "Calm down a minute." Know what
              I mean?

PAT: Daddy, you must be exhausted. The drive to the
              airport.

LILY: Wow, Mum, you're already sounding more
              Australian.

PAT: Well I am an Australian. Underneath all this
              Canadianness.

FERGUS: Oh she is that. You should have seen her as a
              barefooted thing, mustering sheep on horseback.
              Even shooting roos—

JOANNE: You shot kangaroos!

FERGUS: They're a pest on the property.

PAT: It's true.

FERGUS: Well it's lovely to see the bloom of youth on your
              faces. All of you.

Scene Nine

> *(FERGUS's car. Sound: Getting into car. FERGUS starts it and they drive off.)*

ARTHUR: Car runs well.

FERGUS: She's a beaut.

LILY: Are there, like, koala bears just in the trees? Like we have squirrels?

FERGUS: Only in the Outback, love. They wouldn't survive a day in the city, poor dears.

LILY: Shoot, I wanted my very own.

FERGUS: Well we can hold one, in a national park.

JOANNE: Gramps?

FERGUS: Yes, dear?

JOANNE: Do you know where the day goes? That we miss when we fly here from Canada?

FERGUS: Well it disappears.

JOANNE: Like the girls at Hanging Rock? Like that?

FERGUS: Ohhhh yes, that was a strange thing.

JOANNE: But is it? Is it like that?

FERGUS: No. Because a person, in my opinion, never really disappears. No matter how long he's dead. That dateline day, though, that just goes.

PAT: Oh I'm just so happy to be home.

FERGUS: Well move back here then, the lot of you.

PAT: Dad, we would love to, I'm telling you we are so sick of those winters. But Arthur's work, you know.

FERGUS: It's lonesome without you, love.

PAT: We wish you'd come back to Canada and live with us.

FERGUS: Too cold dear, too cold for these bones.

             (Sound: A tropical bird song.)

Scene Ten

             (The house. Sound: FERGUS puts key in lock, opens heavy creaky door.)

FERGUS: Well. There you are.

PAT: House could use a paint job, Dad.

FERGUS: Yes, you're true, love. Been meaning to touch her up.

LILY: Wow. It's so dark.

FERGUS: A relief from the sun, love. The sun can be vicious here.

PAT: I don't mind a dark house one bit. The eyes soon adjust.

JOANNE: I like it dark.

PAT: Dad, my goodness what a lot of newspapers. There must be a over a thousand. Oh my look at this one! 1961!

FERGUS: Yes, yes it's time to throw that one away, I reckon.

             (Sound: They walk into the house.)

PAT: Well if you want our help with them, we're here, Dad.

ARTHUR: How long have you lived here, then, Fergus?

FERGUS: Twenty-five years, I reckon, Art.

PAT: It's the house I was born in. You know that, Art. I haven't been here in twenty-five years. I can't believe it.

JOANNE: I like the wallpaper.

FERGUS: Like that love? Your grandmother, Maura, picked it out. She said it made her happy every day of her life, to look at those blue swirls.

PAT: I remember that. I remember her saying that.

JOANNE: It smells like something like something...

LILY: Smells like an attic. Musty.

PAT: Lillian, that's rude. I'm sorry, Dad, she's a Thunder Bay mall rat.

JOANNE: It smells...familiar.

FERGUS: 'Fraid it needs a bit of elbow grease. But I don't have visitors, you see—not in years, really.

PAT: It's alright Dad, don't even think about it. We'll get at it first thing in the morning.

LILY: Yeah, you should see my room at home, Grampa, it's way worse than this.

PAT: It's a pigsty.

FERGUS: Can I get anybody some carrot juice? Josie next door died of a stroke, last year, left me her juicer. Right there in her will: "Juicer goes to Fergus, next door, who helped my cut me lawn." And I must admit I did.

JOANNE: I would love some carrot juice.

LILY: You're kidding me.

FERGUS: A large glass, Joanne? Or a small one, love.

JOANNE: A large one.

           (Biz: A gasp of pleasure from PAT.)

Scene Eleven

           (The aviary. Sound/Biz: Hundreds of birds in FERGUS's aviary. FERGUS and JOANNE shout

to hear each other above noise. Drop volume of birds after a few lines.)

FERGUS: I got in bad trouble for having this here aviary, love. See I didn't want to worry Maura with it, her so ill, laid up, so I postponed telling her, about the birds, you see. And then one day she came out in her nightie, fancied a passionfruit, I suppose, and she heard the racket. Well she opened the shed doors and three hundred birds flew at her all at once and she dropped to a faint. Broke both her hips. Well she was not pleased, not a bit. I had to promise I'd freed 'em, lied thru my teeth, I did, for I knew she wouldn't be out again, she was far too weak. I couldn't let them go, though, they was precious to me. If you understand what I mean. Having lived my life in the bush. They made the city bearable to me.

JOANNE: Oh yes, grampa, I think they're precious too. They're the most beautiful creatures I've ever seen.

FERGUS: They take to you, love, that's clear. If they didn't, they'd be pecking your head right about now.

           (Sound/Biz: A bird sings and lands on JOANNE's shoulder. She gasps.)

JOANNE: It's on my shoulder.

FERGUS: That's a sure sign. The sitting on the shoulder, a sure sign of acceptance, love. Oh yes, they know you're one of us.

JOANNE: They do?

FERGUS: Absolutely, love. Look at that, two on your head, one on each shoulder, a regular birdgirl.

JOANNE: Gramps? Do you think it bothers them—being locked up and everything?

FERGUS: They can fly away any old time I open the door, dear.

JOANNE: How come they don't?

FERGUS: Perhaps they're afraid.

JOANNE: Of the open air?

FERGUS: Of where they must go.

JOANNE: I know how they feel. Should I stay very still?

FERGUS: Just behave as usual love, as usual. Let them— Oh my goodness—this is the first time I've seen you laughing.

(Sound: Birds becomes louder and louder.)

Scene Twelve

(The kitchen. Sound/Biz: Family eating dinner.)

ARTHUR: Well Fergus that lamb was superlative.

FERGUS: Glad you like it, Arthur. Anybody for more mint jelly?

JOANNE: Yes, I will, Gramps. Oh it's such a nice green.

LILY: I don't believe my eyes. She actually ate it. Like a human.

PAT: Shhh!

FERGUS: Yes, we Aussies love to eat our lamb. Some say it's why we bleat when we talk.

PAT: Bleat?

FERGUS: We talk through the nose, I reckon.

ARTHUR: That's true, to an extent. We Canadians talk from the throat, I believe.

LILLY: You guys are all cracked.

PAT: Lillian, if you can't say anything nice—

ARTHUR: So. I bet you girls are excited about starting at the Sacred Heart tomorrow?

LILY: Yes, Daddy, I've always wanted to go to a Sacred Heart convent.

ARTHUR: Lillian don't be sarcastic please. We don't need that.

JOANNE: I can't wait to meet some Australian kids.

LILY: That's funny, I thought you'd be scared.

JOANNE: What should I be scared of?

LILY: I don't know. Not fitting in. Like in Thunder Bay.

PAT: That was just Thunder Day.

ARTHUR: Of course it was.

LILY: I hope so.

JOANNE: Things might be different here.

PAT: Of course they will.

ARTHUR: Of course they will.

FERGUS: Anyone for a Lamington?

PAT: They look delicious.

JOANNE: Like snow. I love to eat snow.

LILY: Can I have two?

Scene Thirteen

               (FERGUS's living room. Sound: The drone of the television football game.)

LILY: Daddy I'm bored. What's there to do?

ARTHUR: Sit down and watch the game with me, Lil. Come on, keep your old man company.

LILY: But I'm sixteen, Dad, I want to go out.

JOANNE: I'll go for a walk with you, if you want, Lily.

LILY: No, thank you.

PAT: Lil, I know you're used to socializing every night of the week back in Thunder Bay, but don't you think you could just… I don't know, relax, be happy with your family, at least till you make some friends?

LILY: Mum, I just want to go for a walk.

PAT: But where are you going to walk to, Lil?

LILY: I'm going to pick up a guy, Mum. Get laid. I'm horny. Do ya mind? See ya.

(Sound: Door opens, LILY walks out and slams door behind her. Sound: The crickets mate loudly. Sound: Door opens, ARTHUR steps out onto porch.)

ARTHUR: *(Yells.)* Lillian you come back here! You hear me? You come back here right this second.

LILY: *(From sidewalk.)* See ya later!

ARTHUR: Lillian! God is watching you! Remember that!

LILY: Bye Daddy! Love you!

(Sound: ARTHUR comes back inside.)

ARTHUR: Damn her to hell.

FERGUS: Now Artie, you don't mean that.

ARTHUR: Yes I do.

PAT: She is impossible sometimes.

FERGUS: She's restless, our Lil.

PAT: Like a shark.

JOANNE: I think she wants to die.

ARTHUR: Well I'm locking the doors. She'll have to knock till her knuckles are raw.

Scene Fourteen

(The girls' bedroom: Middle of the night. Sound: LILY throws stones at window.)

JOANNE: What's that? Who's there?

             (Sound: JOANNE opens the window.)

             Is somebody there?

LILY: (From outside.) Would you let me in? Asshole's locked me out.

             (Sound: JOANNE leaves the room and walks through the kitchen and opens the back door. Sound: Crickets and nightbirds. Sound: They go back into the house and into their room. Sound: LILY turns the light on.)

JOANNE: Whatja do?

LILY: Got laid. By three different guys. In a UNI dorm. One after the other. Pussy power.

JOANNE: You're lying.

LILY: Why would I lie?

JOANNE: I don't know, Lil. Did you get your period yet?

LILY: Nope.

JOANNE: What are you going to do?

LILY: Boiling hot bath and a bottle of gin. (Moving to adjoining bathroom.) I saw it in a movie.

Scene Fifteen

             (Bathroom. Sound: LILY turns on bath.)

LILY: I've got the gin.

JOANNE: (Following LILY.) Lily! It's not going to work. Besides, you might burn yourself.

LILY: It's my body to burn.

JOANNE: Lily? Where do you think the baby… I mean the fetus…goes? When it dies? Where are they all? All the thousands and thousands of unborn…

LILY: Joanne, get a life.

JOANNE: Yeah.

             (Sound: LILY gets into the bath; JOANNE leaves and shuts the door.)

Scene Sixteen

             (Bedroom.)

LILY: *(Singing through door.)* "Kookaburra sits in the old gum tree-ee. Merry merry king of the bush is he-ee. Laugh, kookaburra laugh, kookaburra." —Oooh that's hot... "gay your life must beeee."

JOANNE: Baby, wherever you're going? I think I'll see you there. I think, I will.

Scene Seventeen

             (JOANNE and LILY in the bathroom.)

LILY: *(Snores in bath.)*

JOANNE: Lil? Lily wake up.

LILY: What?

JOANNE: You fell asleep in the bath.

LILY: I'm freezing.

JOANNE: Why don't you get out now.

LILY: I'm too cold.

             (Sound: JOANNE helps LILY out of the bath.)

             Nothing happened.

JOANNE: We'll find a clinic. I'm sure one of the girls at school will know.

LILY: You'll help me? You'll really help me?

JOANNE:	Of course I will, I'm your sister. Come on now. Here's a towel.

Scene Eighteen

(JOANNE and LILY's bedroom. Sound: FERGUS comes into JOANNE and LILY's bedroom.)

FERGUS:	*(Whispers.)* Joanne, love. Wake up, wake up, then.
JOANNE:	*(Gasps.)* You scared me, Grampa.
FERGUS:	Don't wake Lily. Come out and have a look at the Southern Cross.
JOANNE:	What's that?
FERGUS:	Come and see.
JOANNE:	Alright.

Scene Nineteen

(The garden at night.)

FERGUS:	Right up there. Behind that spire. See? See the cross?
JOANNE:	Oh yeah. We don't have that in Canada.
FERGUS:	Different sky. Different stars.
JOANNE:	Grampa? Do you believe in, like, the stars?
FERGUS:	You mean horoscopes? In the paper?
JOANNE:	Fate.
FERGUS:	It's like a rope around your neck, from the moment you are born. That's what I believe.
JOANNE:	Me too. It's scarey.
FERGUS:	Back to bed, love. Get some rest. Listen, good luck at school tomorrow, love.

JOANNE: Thanks. I'll need it.

FERGUS: Well I'll be thinking of you.

Scene Twenty

> (Schoolyard of the Catholic school: LILY, JOANNE
> and two Australian girls stand in a group. Sound:
> Schoolyard games, laughs, etc., around the group.)

CATH: Listen, Trish. I want you to meet Joanne and Lily.
              They're from America. They're both doing senior.

JOANNE: Canada.

LILY: Same diff.

TRISH: It's close to America, isn't it?

CATH: It's a different country though. I reckon it's like
              saying we're from New Zealand.

JOANNE: Exactly.

LILY: (Imitating JOANNE.) "Exactly."

TRISH
& CATH: (Giggle, not too unkindly.)

LILY: But we don't mind. The States is cool.

JOANNE: We're just as big or bigger even, actually. Except we
              have one tenth of the people.

TRISH: Well pardon our ignorance.

LILY: Hey, you guys probably know more about Canada
              than we know about Australia. I love your shoes.

TRISH: Thanks. I told the nuns I had deformed feet so I
              couldn't wear regulation shoes.

LILY: That is brilliant.

JOANNE: I don't mind the uniform shoes. They're
              comfortable.

CATH: Good old comfortable shoes.

LILY/TRISH/
CATH: *(All laugh.)*

LILY: Yeah, me and my boyfriend, we used to go down to the States all the time.

TRISH: Excellent. What do you do there?

LILY: Shop, drink. The bars are open till, like four. In Canada they close at one.

JOANNE: Big deal. I still like Canada better.

LILY: She's an arse-wipe.

LILY/CATH/
TRISH: *(All laugh.)*

CATH: Arse-wipe. That's a good one. Is that Canadian?

LILY: I guess so. It just means, well, arse-wipe.

TRISH: I like it.

LILY: Right. Hey do any of you smoke?

CATH: I smoke Marlboro.

LILY: Yeah? Gimme one, would ya?

TRISH: Sister Ray would give us the strap if she saw us.

LILY: Come on. Take a chance.

TRISH: We'd be expelled in a minute.

LILY/CATH/
TRISH: *(All giggle again.)*

JOANNE: We don't want to get them in trouble, Lily.

LILY: Of course not, hey anybody got any dope?

JOANNE: She's just kidding.

LILY: I am not, Joanne.

CATH: Do you mean hash? It's easy to get.

JOANNE: She's joking.

LILY: A line of coke, right? I haven't had anything the
            whole time we've been here. I'm goin' nuts.

JOANNE: She doesn't want anything.

TRISH: My brother knows some druggies. But he'd never
            get it for me.

CATH: Besides, it's too dear, isn't it? I've heard it is.

LILY: So introduce me to your brother. Is he cute?

JOANNE: She's kidding.

LILY: Joanne, would you stop being such a suck?

CATH: Suck, I love that.

TRISH: Can't wait to call my brother that.

CATH: What was your school in Canada like? Was it very
            different?

LILY: It was fun. We mainly skipped out, right?

JOANNE: It was awful.

LILY: Yeah, but you were a nerd.

JOANNE: Oh right, thanks. I was a nerd.

LILY: Once a nerd always a nerd. Right guys? You must
            have nerds here.

TRISH: Oh you mean dags. Over there, see those three?

CATH: The one beside her? She has no nose bones. She was
            born that way? And she loves to show you.

TRISH: It's disgusting. And the other one, look at her skin.

CATH: And she never even bothers to wash her face after
            phys-ed.

JOANNE: Are they really that bad?

CATH/TRISH:Yeah.

LILY: Well you know who you're hanging out with, Jo. Why waste any time? You should go over and introduce yourself right now.

LILY/CATH/
TRISH: *(All laugh.)*

JOANNE: Lily. What are you doing?

LILY: *(Laughing.)* What?

JOANNE: Why are you doing this?

LILY: I don't know what you're talking about, Joanne. Oh, by the way. Do either of you know where I could get an abortion?

Scene Twenty-One

(The aviary. Sound: The birds singing.)

JOANNE: Grampa?

FERGUS: Yes, love.

JOANNE: It was just like Thunder Bay.

FERGUS: I had my fears.

JOANNE: And Lily…

FERGUS: She turned on you.

JOANNE: I don't understand it. We were really…close last night.

FERGUS: She's a shark.

JOANNE: She acted like she hated me.

FERGUS: She'll be very sorry for it in years to come, believe me. It'll drive her to drink. To suicide, I believe.

JOANNE: Oh I hope not.

FERGUS: I feel it in my bones, when I look at the girl, love.

JOANNE: You know Grampa, I don't think I want to go back. To school.

FERGUS: I can understand that, love.

JOANNE: To eat lunch alone every day. To be stared at, whispered about. Even the teachers start to sense it, and they stay away. I just don't think I can do it anymore.

FERGUS: I think we should go to the country then. For a long rest.

JOANNE: You mean…like a camping trip?

FERGUS: To the Rock.

JOANNE: Ayers Rock. Oh I'd love to do that, more than anything.

FERGUS: I have to do that. Soon.

(Sound: A bird makes a beautiful, unearthly sound.)

Scene Twenty-Two

(Family dinner in the dining room. Sound: Door opens; LILY enters; door slams behind her.)

ARTHUR: Lillian! Where the hell were you? Why didn't you call!

PAT: Are you trying to make us sick, Lillian?

LILY: I was having an abortion.

FERGUS: Good heavens.

ARTHUR: You were what? WHAT?

PAT: Arthur? Calm down. Honey why don't you sit down.

LILY: *(Teary.)* I just want to go to bed, Mum. I'm very…tired.

ARTHUR: You were WHAT?

FERGUS: Good heavens.

ARTHUR: You have broken your father's heart, Lillian. I want
            you to know that.

PAT: Honey, why didn't you tell us you were pregnant?
            We could have helped you through this.

ARTHUR: As Mother Theresa said in Toronto last year, "If you
            don't want your babies, give them to me." GIVE
            THEM TO ME, she said.

LILY: That's a load of bullshit, Dad. I'm going to bed.

PAT: I'll uh…tuck you in. Come on.

LILY: You know, Dad? I planned with Cath and Trish and
            everybody that after, we would go get drunk at this
            club, and dance, and meet guys? But all I want to do
            is to go to bed. And never get up. In case you were
            interested. *(Crying; moving off.)* I'm so cold,
            Mummy. I'm just so cold.

ARTHUR: *(Moving off.)* You have broken my heart.

            *(Note: JOANNE and FERGUS are left alone;
            FERGUS is short of breath.)*

JOANNE: Grampa? Are you okay?

FERGUS: We must go tonight, Joanne.

JOANNE: Tonight?

FERGUS: To the Rock.

JOANNE: But what about all the camping stuff we need, the
            tents, and…thermos…and…

FERGUS: I'll take care of all that. But we must go by dawn.
            Meet you on the street, love, in front of the house.
            Just before dawn.

JOANNE: Just before dawn. Okay.

FERGUS: *(Out of breath.)* Good on you. A moment on the rock
            and you'll know what you need to know.

            (Sound: "Destiny"/Digeridoo.)

JOANNE: Grampa? You know when birds migrate? Do they, like, have any choice in the matter? Or do they just have to go?

FERGUS: Oh, well. I reckon they just have to go.

JOANNE: But who's…directing them?

FERGUS: I reckon it's God in heaven, or the Devil in hell.

JOANNE: Yeah. Yeah.

Scene Twenty-Three

(Middle of the night in girls' bedroom. Sound: Nightbird, crickets, clock ticking loudly.)

LILY: (Crying.)

JOANNE: Lil?

LILY: Yes.

JOANNE: Are you okay?

LILY: No.

JOANNE: Of course not. It must be so…hard. What you're going through. I can't imagine.

LILY: I just… I didn't expect to feel so…awful.

JOANNE: Listen, Lil. Your baby's spirit is out there somewhere, I know it. And it's just resting now, till it's time to come back.

LILY: Resting?

JOANNE: In…a koala bear, maybe, or a platypus. And then one day, when you are ready to have a baby, the spirit will just swoop down into your belly, and…

LILY: You're weird, Joanne. Don't talk like that.

JOANNE: Okay.

LILY: The fetus is dead. In a garbage bag in the dumpster behind the abortion clinic.

JOANNE:	But you are haunted.
LILY:	I guess you could say that.
JOANNE:	So am I.
LILY:	I only want…to sleep. You know? I don't want to be haunted. I just only want to sleep. *(LILY falls asleep and begins snoring.)*
	(Sound: JOANNE's digital watch alarm starts beeping.)
JOANNE:	*(Int.)* Dawn. Here I go.
	(Sound: JOANNE put on her shoes, picks up her bag.)
LILY:	Joanne?
JOANNE:	Yeah.
LILY:	Where are you going?
	(Silence.)
	Are you coming back? Please come back.
JOANNE:	Of course. Of course I'm coming back.
	(Sound: JOANNE exits the room, and exits the house.)

Scene Twenty-Four

	(Outside. Sound: Rain.)
JOANNE:	Grampa! Grampa!
FERGUS:	Here Joey!
	(Sound: JOANNE runs to meet FERGUS.)
	Joey, you've met Tony.
JOANNE:	You deliver Grampa's mail, don't you?
TONY:	That's a fact, Joanne.

FERGUS: And now he's delivering us.

TONY: Oh well, I've got some time off.

FERGUS: Good turn for a friend.

> (Sound: JOANNE, FERGUS and TONY get in the car, and they take off.)

> (Singing.) "Off we go, into the wild blue yonder..."

Scene Twenty-Five

> (In the Outback. Sound: Midday insects, birds; ominous aboriginal music. Car stops; they get out of the car.)

TONY: Which part of the Rock you want, Fergus?

FERGUS: Away from the people—take us round the shaded part, Tony.

TONY: You're not allowed to go there, Ferg. Blackfellas' secrets.

JOANNE: Why are we not allowed?

FERGUS: Well, the Rock now belongs to the Blackfellas, love. And the shade part is like sacred, but I reckon Jack Wallop give me permission.

JOANNE: The sun...is so bright. I've never felt such heat.

TONY: You sure about this, Ferg. It's awfully bloody hot.

FERGUS: Never been more sure of anything, Tony. We'll be right.

TONY: Long as you know what you're doing, mate. I'll be back in a week then, to pick you up.

FERGUS: Have a nice visit, Tony. Hello to your sister.

> (Sound: TONY takes off in his car.)

JOANNE: He's gone.

FERGUS: A good friend to me, Tony.

JOANNE: Wow. We're really alone. I've never been so alone anywhere.

FERGUS: Not as alone as you think.

JOANNE: What, you mean snakes?

FERGUS: More than that.

JOANNE: You mean ghosts?

FERGUS: I can hear the dead. Can you hear them?

            (Sound: Ghosts; abstracted.)

JOANNE: I can feel them, I think.

Scene Twenty-Six

            (Kitchen at FERGUS's house.)

PAT: Here. Look. I found a note.

ARTHUR: What's it say?

PAT: It says…they've gone…camping. For about a week. In the Outback. Out of Alice. Not to worry.

ARTHUR: Camping? Joanne hates camping.

PAT: "We are very well-equipped, dear Patty, and both excited about our adventure."

ARTHUR: A week! She can't miss a week of school!

PAT: I think it's kind of great. The two of them, off together. This might be just the thing Joanne needs.

ARTHUR: Well I think it's madness. It's bloody dangerous up there.

PAT: Dad knows what he's doing, Artie, he grew up in those parts.

ARTHUR: He's eighty-two years old, Pat. His mind is going.

PAT: Well, what do you think we should do? Do you think we should go look for them?

ARTHUR: What kind of parents would we be if we didn't?

Scene Twenty-Seven

        (Exterior: Ayers Rock. Sound: They are climbing up the rock; Outback ambience.)

FERGUS: *(Out of breath.)* I think you're a natural rock climber, Joanne.

JOANNE: *(Out of breath.)* It's great. I feel great.

FERGUS: I climbed this rock as a boy.

JOANNE: You're sure we won't get arrested?

FERGUS: We belong here, Joey. *(Sound.)*. Don't you feel it?

JOANNE: Yes, I do. Kind of in my stomach.

FERGUS: Here, this is it. Let's have a rest here.

JOANNE: Rest. God. I feel I could lie down and never get up again. Oh. Look at the view.

FERGUS: That is my country.

JOANNE: My country.

FERGUS: Awaiting me.

JOANNE: Yeah. I feel that too.

FERGUS: *(Unwrapping of sandwich.)* Vegemite sandwich?

JOANNE: Thanks. *(She eats.)* I've never been so hungry in my life.

FERGUS: Joanne.

JOANNE: Yes, grampa.

FERGUS: I feel it again. The darkening.

JOANNE: Yes. What's happening? Is it this place?

FERGUS: Can you hear the voices? They're telling me to climb. I'm going to climb.

JOANNE: Climb?

FERGUS: As high as I can go.

JOANNE: Grampa please.

FERGUS: Into the dream.

JOANNE: Grampa, listen, why don't I just take you back to Alice Springs—there must be a hospital.

FERGUS: *(Moving off.)* Don't come after me. I'll see you there, my love.

JOANNE: Oh no. I'm not ready grampa.

            (Sound: FERGUS climbs.)

FERGUS: I'll be waiting for you, love. You'll be right.

JOANNE: I want to go home. I want to go home.

FERGUS: There's no going back, Jo. Like birds migrating, you'll be right.

            (Sound: FERGUS is climbing higher and higher. "Destiny Sound".)

JOANNE: Grampa? Grampa? Please come back? Please.

            (Sound: Very spooky. Kookaburra call.)

Scene Twenty-Eight

            (Exterior Outback. Sound: Police car radio.)

COP: They could be anywhere. We need the tracker to tell us which way.

ARTHUR: Where is this guy, what's taking him so long?

COP: He's on his way, I told you. But listen to me, a tracker is a human being, not a magician. They don't always find what we're looking for. I wouldn't be too optimistic. It is forty-two degrees out there.

PAT: Are you saying…

COP: Listen. You're from Canada. How much hope would you have for an old man and a young girl lost in the what you call it—

LILY: The prairies?

COP: That's it, in say, twenty, thirty below zero snowstorm? How much hope would you have?

Scene Twenty-Nine

(Exterior, near Ayers Rock. Sound: JOANNE's digital watch alarm beeping.)

JOANNE: *(Int.)* Seven hours; I have been walking in this heat for seven hours. My watch will probably still be beeping when I'm just a pile of bones.

(Sound: The sound of a car. Sound: JOANNE runs.)

Heeeeeeelp!! Heeeeeeelp!!

(Sound: Another car goes by.)

Hey!! Wait!! Pleeeease!!

(Sound: The car pulls up ahead.)

(Int.) An angel of mercy, an angel. Hi! Thank you for stopping.

DRIVER: *(From inside car.)* No problem. Get in.

(Sound: "Destiny" as she gets in.)

Scene Thirty

(Interior of car.)

DRIVER: Where ya headed?

JOANNE: The nearest phone, please. Do you have anything to drink?

DRIVER: Sure.

            (Sound: He opens a can.)

            Ginger ale alright?

JOANNE: Oh thank you, thank you.

            (Sound: She drinks.)

            I've never tasted anything so good in my life.

DRIVER: That's Canada Dry.

JOANNE: Huh. That's funny. I'm Canadian.

DRIVER: I know.

JOANNE: Oh yeah?

            (Sound: She continues to drink.)

            How'd you know?

DRIVER: The way ya talk. I could tell right off.

JOANNE: Yeah?

DRIVER: What happened, you get lost?

JOANNE: Well I was…yeah, I was on a hike and I got lost.

DRIVER: Didn't anybody tell you the country 'round here is deadly?

JOANNE: Well, I had someone who knew his way but… You're not from around here either, are you?

DRIVER: What makes ya say that?

JOANNE: Well you don't talk…Australian, either. I mean your accent. It's more—Canadian.

DRIVER: What makes ya say that?

JOANNE: It just is. You roll your "r's" and…well you're not American.

DRIVER: You got a good ear.

JOANNE: Oh yeah? Where are from?

DRIVER: A piece of heaven called Thunder Bay. It's in the middle of nowhere.

             (Sound: "Destiny Sound".)

             I guess that's why I like the north here.

JOANNE: I don't believe it.

DRIVER: You're from Thunder Bay too.

JOANNE: How did you know?

DRIVER: I seen you around. D'you go to TBCVI?

JOANNE: Yeah. Yeah I did. I don't remember you.

DRIVER: I wasn't there long.

JOANNE: So. You live here now.

DRIVER: Best place in the world. First place I feel I belong.

JOANNE: Why do you think that is?

DRIVER: It's the desert. Miles and miles of nothing, you know? No water, no trees, and then suddenly, there's a carpet snake, moving along. All alone, but it doesn't bother him. He just... You finished that off pretty quick. Want some of this drink I got?

JOANNE: Sure, what is it?

DRIVER: Passiona. I love everything passionfruit, it's my greatest taste.

JOANNE: That's nice.

DRIVER: Can't get that in Canada.

JOANNE: No. No you can't.

DRIVER: No, you can't.

Scene Thirty-One

> *(In the Dream Time. Sound: FERGUS flying...whooshing through the air like a great bird, plus flute.)*

FERGUS: *(Int.)* Oh this is everything I imagined, this vanishing, flying, over desert, flying free, just like the dreams, what a terrible weight a human body was, a terrible...

> *(Sound: FERGUS's birds from the aviary—a great clamour.)*

My friends from the shed, hullo, hullo, my lovely birdies how good of you to come and guide me to wherever I'm going wherever...

> *Sound: The birds now sound very agitated, upset.)*

What is it, my friends? Has something alarmed you?

> *(Sound: "Destiny Sound." Sound: Flying, whooshing through the air, the clamour of upset birds.)*

Scene Thirty-Two

> *(Interior of car. Sound: Car slows to a stop.)*

JOANNE: Why are we stopping?

DRIVER: I just thought you might want to relax.

JOANNE: Isn't it too hot to stop?

DRIVER: That's just it, Joanne. I'm gettin' too hot. I think you know what I mean.

JOANNE: No. I don't know what you mean.

DRIVER: Didn't anyone tell you that wearing little shorts is gonna get you in trouble?

JOANNE: I'm wearing shorts because it's hot. Outside.

DRIVER: Them nice white skinny legs. Just like a little girlie, eh? Like a schoolgirl.

JOANNE: Can we keep driving please. I really have to get to a phone.

DRIVER: Like to have them legs wrapped around my neck, Joanne.

JOANNE: Well, um, I'm really flattered, but my parents are probably out looking for me and...

DRIVER: I don't like chicks who mouth off, okay? So just keep it shut and we'll be fine. I like quiet girls.

JOANNE: Listen, please listen to me, and I won't say anything more. When I climbed on the rock, I felt something I hadn't felt for a long time. I think my grandfather knew too, he knew that when you're on the rock you must pick between death and life and I want life. I'm gonna fight through the loneliness and the whispers and the not being invited, everything's going to be okay, and I just want a chance, okay? I want to go back to Canada, and, and, and...

DRIVER: I been waitin' for you all my life, Joanne.

JOANNE: No. No you haven't.

DRIVER: I am your destiny. I am. You know it, I know it, all the kids at your school knew it. That's why they didn't want nothin' to do with you, Joe. They smelled me on ya. I owned ya, ever since you come into this world. Like the Canada Geese must fly down to Florida, you flown down to me. My little snowbird. We're just the same, you and me, we been headin' towards this moment all our lives. All our stupid lives. This is the only moment gonna give meaning to our lives, gonna leave us a headline. Cold. Oooh, look at them passionfruit lips. I don't think you never been kissed, Joanne. I think you been waitin' for me to kiss ya right. Gimme a wet snowy kiss. Come on. Come on, baby.

JOANNE: *(Trying to bide her time, not anger him.)* Okay. Okay.

(She kisses him quickly on the cheek. Sound: Double "Destiny Sound".)

There's a kiss. You're very nice, a very nice, I think, inside, a kind person, aren't you? I'm sure you're a really kind person. Now please, can we just...

(Sound: DRIVER laughs and laughs. His laughter turns into: "Destiny Sound" and a sound/animal equivalent of human violence—indicating that the DRIVER is killing JOANNE. Screams.)

Scene Thirty-Three

                        (Exterior, near Ayers Rock.)

LILY: *(Gasps, almost choking.)*

PAT: Lily, are you alright?

LILY: Something terrible is happening to Jo right now, this minute.

ARTHUR: In the name of God, Lily. I don't want to hear from you again.

LILY: And it's all my fault.

                (Sound: The same sound equivalent of human violence under FERGUS flying.)

Scene Thirty-Four

                        (Interior of car.)

JOANNE: *(Making sounds of fear; the sounds are weaker and weaker.)*

DRIVER: I'm ice and I'm snow, snow inside your sweetness you ripened for me all your life little passionfruit. Ooh yeah, yeah, yeah, some winters back home icicles'd be so bad, remember? Remember? They'd kill one, two, three people pierce 'em right through the head, the chest, the sweet, sweet...

JOANNE: *(Screams final scream.)*

Scene Thirty-Six

(Interior of jeep, driving.)

PAT: I'm not leaving here till we find them. I'm just not.

COP: It's been two days, Miss. Fuel won't last.

PAT: I'm not leaving here till we find them. At least their remains.

ARTHUR: I'm with my wife. At least we have to find the bones.

TRACKER: Vultures'd take the innards. Dingoes'd take the bones.

LILY: But isn't the rock magic? Don't your people— believe in some kind of...

TRACKER: The only kind of magic rocks I know are the ones you send away for ninety-nine cents on the back of a *Phantom* comic. A rock's a rock, if you ask me.

LILY: What's that thing over there? With all the vultures on it?

COP: Well. I guess we oughta go have a look...eh, Nathan? The rest of you—stay here. You'll be right.

(Sound: Stops the vehicle, TRACKER gets out.)

ARTHUR: It's probably a kangaroo carcass. A...what do they call them here, a Joey.

PAT: I'm sure it is. Of course. Horrible things don't happen in our family. They never have.

ARTHUR: I'm sure they're just fine.

PAT: Of course they're fine, Arthur. Do I hear some doubt in your voice?

ARTHUR: No. Not really. No.

(*Sound: The birds and the murmuring spirits including JOANNE and FERGUS hover over the group.*)

LILY: Do you guys hear voices? I hear these voices, like church, like the choir in Thunder Bay at St. Pat's.

ARTHUR: That's Outback birds, Lil, look up.

PAT: I wish they would just stop that racket for a moment.

(*Sound: The birds clamour and then pass over. The COP and TRACKER are a hundred yards away, standing over the bodies. The sound of vultures.*)

COP: Well, looks like the two of 'em. Died wrapped around each other.

TRACKER: Two days dead I'd say. Dropped with heat. Suffered heart attack. Birds got the rest.

COP: Yeah. Poor fellow. Poor girl.

TRACKER: Yeah. Poor girl. Poor family.

COP: Poor us. Having to hand out the hankies.

TRACKER: Part of the job, Frank? It's what we're paid for.

COP: Bloody hell. It's never enough, is it?

TRACKER: No. Never enough.

(*Sound: "Destiny Sound".*)

PAT: I'm sure they're just fine. I'm the mother. I'm the daughter. I would know.

LILY: Oh Mum, stop talking like that. Would everyone please stop. When it comes right down to it, you don't know anything. Not one of us knows a goddamned thing.

(*Sound: "Destiny Sound".*)

The End.

HOW TO MAKE LOVE TO AN ACTOR

GEORGE F. WALKER

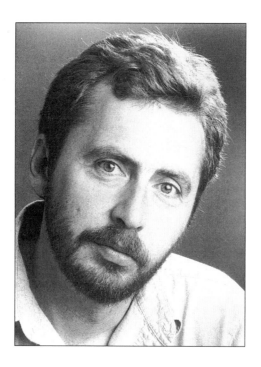

George F. Walker was born and raised in Toronto's east-end, the setting for many of his plays. While working as a cab driver in the early 1970s, Walker saw a poster for Factory Theatre Lab requesting original scripts. He wrote *Prince of Naples* and with that play began a long and fruitful association with Factory. Walker was playwright-in-residence at that theatre from 1971 to 1976 and Artistic Director in 1978-79. Among his works to premiere there were *Love and Anger*, *Criminals in Love* and *Theatre of the Film Noir*. He was also associated with Toronto Free Theatre, and spent a year as playwright-in-residence at the New York Shakespeare Festival.

Walker's work has been performed around the world, and most of his plays have been published. He has received many honours, including the Governor General's Award for *Nothing Sacred* and *Criminals in Love*; Chalmers Canadian Play Awards for *Escape from Happiness*, *Love and Anger*, *Nothing Sacred*, *Criminals In Love*, *Theatre of the Film Noir* and *Zastrozzi*; and Dora Outstanding Play awards for *Escape From Happiness*, *Love and Anger* and *Nothing Sacred*.

Walker has also written five original plays for radio. They include two yet-to-be-aired works, *How To Make Love To An Actor, Part 2: The Green Room* for *Sunday Showcase*, and *The Favour*, a CBC-BBC co-production.

How To Make Love to an Actor was first broadcast on *Sunday Showcase*, on October 1, 1995, with the following cast:

WILLIE .... Graham Greene

JESS .... Brenda Robins

SANDY .... Lenore Zann

ROSS .... Michael McManus

Producer .... James Roy

Production Assistant .... Nina Callaghan

Recording Engineer .... Greg DeClute

Sound Effects .... Joe Hill

Casting Director .... Linda Grearson

Script Editor .... Dave Carley

Scene One

(*A large rehearsal room. Sound: Some shuffling of feet.*)

WILLIE: (*A loud sigh.*)

(*Sound: A chair moves a bit.*)

JESS: So…so do I do this forever? …Well?

WILLIE: (*Sighs.*)

JESS: Why are you sighing, Willie. I'm just asking a question. I mean I do this and then I do…what? Speak? Or what? Do you tell me when to speak. Or what? I just wait. Until…when. When I feel like speaking…or…what.

WILLIE: You know something? I don't get it.

JESS: Yeah. Get what.

WILLIE: Your problem. The problem you have understanding a simple suggestion.

JESS: Come on. I just want to know how long I'm supposed to—

WILLIE: It's not about how long. If you say it that way it sounds like you're being punished.

JESS: Okay, forget it. I was just—

WILLIE: But I guess that's the thing though. You think it's some kind of punishment.

JESS: Okay, okay! Forget it. I'll do it. Just…let me do it.

(*Sound: A chair moves.*)

Can you ask her to stop doing that with her chair? Scraping her chair along the floor like that.

WILLIE: Sandy.

SANDY: Sorry.

JESS: *(Making little groaning noises.)*

WILLIE: What are you doing.

JESS: Whatya mean.

WILLIE: What's all that rolling shit you're doing with your neck.

JESS: Relaxation. I'm trying to get relaxed.

WILLIE: Who asked you to get relaxed.

JESS: No one asked me to get relaxed. I feel like getting relaxed. It might help.

WILLIE: Look. Just lower your head and talk to the floor. You know your lines? You've picked a speech?

JESS: Yeah. Do you want to know what it's from?

WILLIE: I don't give a shit what it's from. I just want you to do it.

JESS: To the floor.

WILLIE: Yes. To the floor.

JESS: Right.

(Sound: Feet shuffling.)

WILLIE: *(Sighs.)*

JESS: Okay. I need to hear it from you again. Why am I doing this.

WILLIE: Jesus. Come on, Jess.

JESS: No, no. Just tell me once more. Because, okay, I don't understand. I don't get it. I'm trying but... Okay look, I can talk to the floor. I can do that. I can do it all night—

SANDY: Starting when.

                (Sound: SANDY moves her chair a bit.)

JESS: Have you got something to say to me.

SANDY: I just said it.

JESS: I meant have you got something to say of any value. Not just a sarcastic little quip. Something that might actually help me understand why I'm acting to a floor.

SANDY: Maybe if you just get on with it, if you just do it, you might find that you understand why he asked you to do it.

JESS: I think it's better if he just tells me. You know like one human to another. If he just passes along the information.

WILLIE: I already told you.

JESS: I didn't understand what you told me. So I want you to tell me again. But in a way I understand.

WILLIE: Jesus.

JESS: No, look. Really. I'm gonna be doing a speech to the floor. It's kinda embarrassing. I just want to make sure I've got the reason I'm doing it nailed down. So there can be value in it. Okay. Here's the thing. I'm supposed to talk to the floor to keep me from doing something. What is it again. What's the thing you don't want me to do again.

WILLIE: Perform.

JESS: Yeah. Right. I'm not supposed to perform.

WILLIE: You remember now?

JESS: I never forgot. I never said I forgot. I just don't understand.

WILLIE: Jesus.

JESS: Okay. I'm not supposed to "perform". Can I "act".

WILLIE: What are you getting at?

JESS: What's the difference again.

WILLIE: You don't know the difference?

JESS: I never said I didn't know. I just want to know what *you* think it is. I mean the hell with what I know. You're the teacher. I just want to do it so it conforms to *your* beliefs. Because, hey, I just want to do it once, you know. I want to do it once right and never have to do it again.

WILLIE: Okay. That's it. *(Moving off.)* I'm outta here.

JESS: Where are you going. I just want you to explain yourself. You don't want me to "perform". I just want you to tell me what that means to you. Does it have anything to do with silly facial expressions or anything.

WILLIE: *(At the door.)* Class is over. Goodbye.

             (Sound: Door opens, closes. Pause.)

SANDY: *(Sighs.)*

             (Sound: Moves her chair.)

JESS: What are you looking at, Sandy?

SANDY: Right now, Jess? …You.

JESS: Really.

SANDY: I pay money for these classes.

JESS: So what. So do I.

SANDY: You eat time. I don't get my share of his time. You eat it all.

JESS: Hey. I had a problem. I didn't understand what he was talking about.

SANDY: He was talking about good acting.

JESS: "Good acting". What the hell is that? I just wanted him to explain why I was doing that stupid exercise.

SANDY:	He told you. You don't listen.
JESS:	He doesn't make sense. He talks in code. "Don't perform." "Keep it personal." "Talk to the floor." Who could understand that?
SANDY:	I did.
JESS:	Bullshit. You just think you did. You think you understand the code. But you don't really. Nobody does. That's why this business is such crap. I'm just looking for some practical advice here. A little...sound judgment.
SANDY:	So get a therapist.
JESS:	I've got a therapist.
SANDY:	Do you drive him nuts too.
JESS:	It's not a "him". It's a "her". No wonder you're under this guy's spell here. You're unevolved.
SANDY:	Maybe... But I can act.
JESS:	Yeah. (*Moves off.*) You're a frigging genius. (*Stops.*) You're brilliant in that Toyota commercial.
SANDY:	Go to hell.
JESS:	Asshole.
	(*Sound: Door opens, as:*)
WILLIE:	(*Comes back into room, meets JESS, moves on.*) Ah, hi...are you leaving.
JESS:	Yeah.
WILLIE:	I was coming back...to you know... But you're leaving.
JESS:	Right.
WILLIE:	You don't want to keep working? ...Because I've decided to give you another chance.
JESS:	That's big of you. (*Moves off.*) Now get out of my way.

(Sound: Door slams.)

WILLIE: Jesus... What do you think her problem is. Is it me? Maybe I just rub her the wrong way.

SANDY: I don't want to talk about her.

WILLIE: I was just trying to help her. I think she's worth the effort. She's got a lot of stuff going on there. What do you think.

SANDY: I gotta go. Where's my coat?

WILLIE: On your chair. What's wrong?

SANDY: I gotta go. It's time...to go.

WILLIE: We can work. You wanna work?

SANDY: No. I wanna go.

WILLIE: Look don't get in a snit. Okay I know I pretty much ignored you today. But Jess and I have a thing to work out. If I'm gonna be able to help her I had to bring it to the surface. Find out what it is...the thing...

SANDY: Now *that's* code. *That* I recognize. And it's definitely code.

WILLIE: Code? What are you—

SANDY: You had her doing that floor thing...for an hour. I'd have gotten pissed off too.

WILLIE: I was just trying—

SANDY: It was about power. You're trying to break her. Like she's a horse or something. It's bullshit, Willie. We expect better from you.

WILLIE: So that's what you think... You tell her that... That you agreed with her. You make some kind of pact or something.

SANDY: Look. I gotta go. I've got an audition.

WILLIE: Yeah? For what?

SANDY: I told you. That slasher movie.

WILLIE: Come on. You can't audition for that.

SANDY: It's a job.

WILLIE: Yeah but it's vile. The word's out about that script and it's supposed to be...vile.

SANDY: It's a job. It's important to me that I think about acting as a job.

WILLIE: That's because you're afraid to really commit.

SANDY: No. It's because I'm afraid of starving to death.

(Starts towards him.)

WILLIE: Where are you going?

SANDY: Whatya mean where am I going? I just told you.

WILLIE: Now?

SANDY: Yeah.

WILLIE: You don't wanna work?

SANDY: *(Close to him.)* Can't.

WILLIE: Because I thought we could work now. And then later...you know...do it. *(Very close to her.)*

SANDY: Willie. Get out of the way.

WILLIE: Or we could forget the work...and you know...do it now... Jesus, you've got great...

SANDY: Look, this isn't going to happen now.

WILLIE: It's gotta happen now.

SANDY: Maybe later. I'll come by your place. Tonight.

WILLIE: *(He is kissing her face.)* Tonight's okay. But so is now. Put your hand on me.

SANDY: No! I have to go. I've probably got a shot at this part.

WILLIE: They just want you for your body. They'll probably

make you wear something slutty. You got anything slutty?

SANDY: I've got a red thing.

WILLIE: What's it like.

SANDY: It's...red... Short. Push-up bra.

WILLIE: *(His breathing has become heavier.)* Well, you should wear it for me sometime.

SANDY: I could wear it to the audition. Then come over to your place after.

WILLIE: Tell me what it looks like now. I...need to hear about it now.

SANDY: I gotta go.

WILLIE: Where.

SANDY: To the audition.

WILLIE: What audition.

SANDY: *(Moving off.)* Jesus.

WILLIE: What are you doing.

SANDY: Leaving.

WILLIE: Really.

SANDY: Yes.

WILLIE: But I need you to stay. You really leaving?

SANDY: Yes.

WILLIE: Why.

SANDY: Jesus.

(Sound: She leaves. Door closes.)

WILLIE: *(Weakly.)* Come back. Come on. Really. *(Sighs.)*

(Music:)

Scene Two

> (*Waiting room. Sound/Biz: A bit of chair shuffling. Some mumbling and pages being flipped.*)

JESS &
SANDY: (*Reading to themselves. The odd word is spoken aloud.*)

SANDY: (*Laughs.*)

> (*Pause.*)

> (*Laughs again.*)

JESS: What?

SANDY: What? I didn't say anything.

JESS: You laughed. Was that a laugh.

SANDY: Yeah.

JESS: Are we reading the same thing here. Let me see it. Hold it up.

> (*Sound: Script held up.*)

SANDY: There. Happy?

JESS: It's the same script.

SANDY: That's right.

JESS: So where's the laugh.

SANDY: What.

JESS: You laughed… Twice. What page are you on.

SANDY: Thirty-two.

> (*Sound: JESS flips pages.*)

JESS: (*Reads the page really fast.*) There's nothing funny on this page.

SANDY: When she says "Come on, it wasn't my fault."

JESS: She's talking about being raped, Sandy. What's funny about that.

SANDY: She's a hooker.

JESS: Jesus Christ. You're sick... So where's the second laugh.

SANDY: Same place.

JESS: You laughed at that twice? Sick.

SANDY: Maybe you don't have a very good sense of humour. My agent told me this was a comedic role.

JESS: You trust your agent.

SANDY: With my life.

JESS: Sad. Look. This character is in three scenes. One when she's being raped and beaten. One when she's being interrogated by the cops. And one when the guy who raped her comes back and takes a machete to her. Three scenes and none of them are funny. Take my word for it.

SANDY: Well, it depends on how it's done.

JESS: What were you like before you got into this business. Were you always like this. Or have you made some huge accommodation.

SANDY: I keep a positive attitude. I behave like a professional. If I'm advised that a role has comic potential I take that advice seriously.

JESS: But... But it doesn't. You were given bad advice.

SANDY: You're a political person, aren't you.

JESS: What's that supposed to mean.

SANDY: It means you've got a point of view or something. You do a lot of small theatre work, don't you?

JESS: Yeah. So?

SANDY: So that probably explains your point of view.

JESS: Which is?

SANDY: Limited.

JESS: What the hell do you know about my work in the theatre.

SANDY: I've seen you in those plays.

JESS: Which ones?

SANDY: All of them. I've seen all your work. I think you're very good. You're funny and…touching.

JESS: Really.

SANDY: Oh yeah. As an actress in those little plays you shine. I think you're a really messed-up person though. And a self-righteous pain in the ass. Also I think you're getting worse. We've been taking Willie's class for, what, three months now. And you get worse every time.

JESS: In what way "worse".

SANDY: As a person, mostly. But also as an actor. You're getting tighter and tighter by the minute. What's wrong. What's wrong with you anyway. Someone die?

JESS: I beg your pardon.

SANDY: You don't want advice from me. But here it is, anyway. You can't come to auditions like this with a point of view. It's just a job.

JESS: You're the one with the point of view. You've decided you're auditioning for a boffo comedy about rape and dismemberment.

SANDY: I'm just following advice. You've decided you're auditioning for a piece of shit.

JESS: It is a piece of shit.

SANDY: The movie-going audience will make that decision.

JESS: Why can't I make it too.

SANDY:	You can. But you'll blow the audition.
JESS:	Maybe I want to blow it. Maybe that's why I'm here. To blow the audition in a very spectacular way. Maybe it's my way of saying screw you to this whole crappy business.
SANDY:	*(Sighs.)* Politics.
JESS:	Jesus.

(Sound: Door opens.)

ROSS:	*(Comes in.)* Okay, ah... Sandy?
SANDY:	That's me.
ROSS:	Great. Come on in. And...ah... You must be...ah...ah...
JESS:	The brunette.
ROSS:	What?
JESS:	I'm the brunette hooker. She's the blonde hooker. We're here to give you a real choice. Two types. A blonde type. A brunette type. Her or me. Whoever.
ROSS:	*(Whispers to SANDY.)* What's her problem.
SANDY:	Beats me.
JESS:	I gotta go now. I'm late for something. I'd like to stay. I really would. But I gotta go. I'm expected somewhere. People are waiting for me. Serious people. They're waiting for me and I gotta go meet them and together we're going to do something serious together.
ROSS:	*(To SANDY.)* Do you know what she's talking about?
SANDY:	A play, maybe. Maybe she's going to rehearse a play.
JESS:	A play? No way. Something serious. Gardening. Or street sweeping. Or maybe filing. Yeah, a useful activity like filing. Something that makes sense.

(Moving off.) I gotta go, really. See ya.

(Sound: Door opens, closes.)

ROSS: Do you think she's coming back.

SANDY: Beats me.

ROSS: So what was that. Was she trying to impress me or something. Was that some kind of audition trick.

SANDY: I don't know.

ROSS: If it was, it didn't work… *(Moving off.)* Come on in.

Scene Three

(Medium-sized rehearsal room. Sound: Door closes.)

ROSS: *(Moving on.)* So ah…here we are. You can sit over there.

SANDY: *(Moving on.)* There's no one else here.

(Sound: Chair scrape.)

ROSS: No.

SANDY: No one else coming? No director?

ROSS: I'm the director.

SANDY: No producer?

ROSS: I'm the producer… Okay. So we're just going to read a little. Okay?

SANDY: Sure.

ROSS: Maybe later we'll put a bit of something on video. But now we'll just read the second scene. You've got all three there?

(Sound: Paper shuffling.)

SANDY: Yeah.

ROSS: Okay. Good. But we're just doing the second one. That's with the two cops. I'll read them both. I'll just switch back and forth. I won't, you know, "indicate" which one or anything.

SANDY: Yeah.

ROSS: Okay. So let's—

SANDY: Oh. I forgot. I've got something in my purse…here.

                (Sound: Zipper. Rummaging in purse. Rustle of dress.)

ROSS: What's that.

SANDY: It's my red dress. I brought it to you know…put on.

ROSS: So why didn't you…

SANDY: You want me to.

ROSS: Well, I—

                (Sound: Rustle of dress.)

SANDY: It's…tight. Very revealing. I think I'll just hold it. Okay. I'll hold it like this… Or maybe this way is better.

ROSS: Whatever. Can we read now.

SANDY: I guess.

ROSS: Okay. So let's just start…

SANDY: Sorry. Yeah. Ah…just one… Do you think any of this is you know…funny.

ROSS: What. The situation?

SANDY: No, the script.

ROSS: The script? No, not really.

SANDY: Because I was told you were looking for a kind of comic take on it.

ROSS: Who told you that.

SANDY: Well, I... Jess...

ROSS: Jess. Who's Jess.

SANDY: You know, that other actor who was out in reception with me. She said she thought you were—

ROSS: Sounds like she was messing with your mind. It's not a comedy.

SANDY: No... No, it's not a comedy. I never thought that. But...well...

ROSS: What?

SANDY: It's not a comedy. But it is kind of outrageous.

ROSS: I'm sorry...

SANDY: Outrageous. You know? Too much. So you could have a take on it that...you know...showed that. Showed that you knew that.

ROSS: I still don't see—

SANDY: Well, it's so...you know, abusive. This girl is just shit on here. She's...like... It's like some sick male fantasy. So if you did it with, well, maybe some irony or something it might help people swallow the—

ROSS: If you don't like the part you don't have to read for it.

SANDY: Well, I didn't say—

ROSS: What's the problem here. If there's a problem for you in this you can just walk away. No harm done.

SANDY: Yeah. Well. You see that's not true. First of all, I can't just walk away. This is how I make a living. I'm just looking for a way to do it I can...justify.

ROSS: What the hell are you talking about. Who are they sending me here. You sound like that other one.

SANDY: Now that's not fair. She wasn't even willing to audition.

ROSS:	Look, do you want to read this thing or not.
SANDY:	Can I make it funny.
ROSS:	No.
SANDY:	Then I guess not.
ROSS:	You don't want to read? Is that what you're saying.
SANDY:	If you're saying I have to do it straight. All this beaten, abused, sad, pathetic victim stuff.
ROSS:	Wait a minute—
SANDY:	Well, that's the choice. You take away the comedy, which in this case would just be a kind of self-awareness for this character. A way to let the audience know that she knows she's just some kind of thing. Some sick male fantasy thing. If you take that away then I can't do it. I have to leave.
ROSS:	So leave.
SANDY:	Okay. But it's too bad. Because I could have made her funny. And that would have made your movie better.
ROSS:	Says you.
SANDY:	Yeah. But I'm right... So it was nice meeting you.

(*Sound: Chair scrape as she stands. Pause.*)

ROSS:	Look, put your hand down. I don't want to shake your hand.
SANDY:	Why not. I'm just trying to be professional here.
ROSS:	A professional would have just read the scene.
SANDY:	Really?... You have people who do that? You've had women read this character already?
ROSS:	Lots of them.
SANDY:	And no one mentioned the way it's written.
ROSS:	No one.

SANDY: Really? *(Starts off.)* How about that. That's amazing.

                (Sound: She leaves. Door closes. Music:)

Scene Four

                (Large rehearsal room.)

WILLIE: Go ahead, quit. I don't care if you quit. I thought we were meeting here to work. If you wanted to quit why didn't you just tell me on the phone. I rent this rehearsal room by the hour.

JESS: I wanted to tell you face to face. Besides I'm not quitting. I'm leaving.

WILLIE: Quitting, leaving—what's the difference.

JESS: Well, quitting makes it sound like I've failed and given up. When actually the truth is, you've failed and I'm just moving on.

WILLIE: Look I thought what happened yesterday was just... Look you can blame me if you want. I don't care. I'm just here to help actors get better.

JESS: Yeah, well, you didn't help me, Willie.

WILLIE: You didn't want me to help you. You were just looking for someone to blame.

JESS: Blame for what.

WILLIE: Your ungenerous anxieties.

JESS: What the hell does that mean. My "ungenerous anxieties". Can't you just talk like a human being. You talk like the head of some cult. Talk like what you're paid to be. An acting teacher.

WILLIE: Okay. You're trying to get at something here. What is it.

JESS: I'm not trying to "get at" anything. I'm telling you.

WILLIE: What are you telling me.

JESS: I'm telling you you're a lousy teacher who talks in code because you think the code gives you power.

WILLIE: Bullshit. You're the one with the…code. You act with a code. You act in code.

JESS: Jesus.

WILLIE: Ah just go away. I thought you were leaving. Leave.

JESS: I'll leave when I want to leave. I…don't act in code. What the hell does that mean.

WILLIE: You work from the part of you that's only connected to your own immediate needs. You're not connected to anyone you work with or anyone who might be watching you work.

JESS: And I'm supposed to understand that crap. That "connection" crap. That's supposed to be "insightful" right.

WILLIE: You want it clearer? Okay. You're a selfish bitch.

JESS: What did you call me?

WILLIE: I called you a selfish bitch. And you are. You're a goddamn self-obsessed smart-assed obnoxious paranoid selfish bitch.

JESS: You asshole!

                (Biz: She attacks him.)

WILLIE: Hey. What the… Hey get away from me. Hey. That hurt.

                (Biz: They struggle. Music:)

Scene Five

                (Restaurant. Sound: Moderately busy background.)

SANDY: Hey. Jess. Over here… Jess. Jess!

JESS: *(Moving closer.)* Hello.

SANDY: You wanna join me?

JESS: No.

SANDY: Come on. Join me. Come on.

JESS: *(Moving on.)* You're eating salad. I don't want to eat salad. I want to drink alcohol. I want to drink lots of alcohol. What's that drink?

SANDY: Milkshake.

JESS: I don't want to sit with you. You're drinking a milkshake. I mean, get serious.

SANDY: I could get rid of the milkshake.

JESS: And the salad?

SANDY: Sure.

JESS: Okay then.

(Sound: JESS sits. Dishes being moved.)

SANDY: Okay. There. Table's clear. A fresh start. Okay?

JESS: Okay. *(She whistles.)*

SANDY: What are you doing?

JESS: I'm getting a waiter. What do you want.

SANDY: I'll have what you're having.

JESS: Scotch. I'm gonna have a scotch.

SANDY: Vodka's better. I mean it is only three in the afternoon.

JESS: I don't know what that means. But okay. Vodka. See? I'm not hard to please.

SANDY: I always knew that. You're a pussycat.

JESS: I'm sorry about what I said about your Toyota commercial.

SANDY:	Me too. I mean you really hurt my—
JESS:	Jesus. What's wrong with him.
SANDY:	Who?
JESS:	The waiter. Why is he ignoring me?
SANDY:	He's busy at the cash register. Also, maybe he doesn't like being whistled for like a dog.
JESS:	I wouldn't have to whistle if he wasn't ignoring me. You know why he's ignoring me? Yesterday I asked him to stop looking down my shirt. I was polite about it. But I wanted him to stop. So today...look at him, he's ignoring me. Tomorrow he'll be openly hostile. Maybe some night soon he'll be waiting outside my apartment with a razor blade. Or some acid to toss in my face. Jesus. What ya have to do to get by... When's it gonna stop being like that.
SANDY:	I think you should calm down.
JESS:	Look... I think I'm going to cry. Do you want me to leave.
SANDY:	No. I don't want you to leave. But maybe we could just—
JESS:	(Bursts into tears.) I mean... I can't... I mean what do they want from me... Jesus... Oh Jesus do they want to break me... Okay I'm broken. I'm crying. Look at me! I'm crying. I never cry. Never! Jesus! Hell... Shit.

> (Music: Should come in during above speech and rise above her voice... Then fade into...)

Scene Six

> (Medium rehearsal room. Sound: Door closes.)

ROSS:	Just take one of those chairs.
WILLIE:	Sure.

(Sound: A bit of chair shuffling.)

ROSS: I've seen your work man, you're a really good actor.

WILLIE: Thanks.

ROSS: I'm glad you came in. When I asked for you they told me you were retired or something.

WILLIE: I teach. But I'm not... Who told you I was retired. My agent?

ROSS: I can't remember.

WILLIE: Oh... Well, I'm not. I still act.

ROSS: That's great. It would be a loss if you didn't.

WILLIE: Sure.

ROSS: No, I mean that. A loss. So...so okay you're reading for Jonathan the serial murderer. You knew that?

WILLIE: No.

ROSS: They didn't tell you.

WILLIE: Who?

ROSS: Your agent.

WILLIE: No, she just said you wanted to see me.

ROSS: I wanted to see you for Jonathan the...serial...murderer. Yeah?

WILLIE: Yeah. ...What?

ROSS: Any thoughts?

WILLIE: I...haven't read the script.

ROSS: Ahhh. Why not, man.

WILLIE: I wasn't given one.

ROSS: That's a mistake. You should have been given a script. We told your agent we were serious about you. She should have asked for a script.

WILLIE: You made an offer?

ROSS: Not "offer-serious". Not yet. But serious enough to let you read the script… Someone messed up. It was probably your agent.

WILLIE: I'll ask her…

ROSS: Look, I don't care. Do you want to read cold?

WILLIE: You want me to read. I thought it was an interview.

ROSS: An interview, an audition, whatever. Look, we're serious about you… You don't audition, right. I mean I can understand how you—

WILLIE: I don't mind auditioning. I just thought it was an interview.

ROSS: Look, my gut says give you the part. It really does. But… I'm a little nervous. You know, it's a big part…it's *the* part, really. And okay, you've done three features. Look, I know your work on stage. I've seen it. I'm a fan. But just three features. And *the* part.

WILLIE: I'll read for it. I'm not hung up about it.

ROSS: Look, suppose I just told you about the guy first. No, let me do that first. Okay?

WILLIE: Sure.

ROSS: Okay. He's sick. That's obvious. He kills people at random in very nasty ways. This is a ninety-five minute feature and he kills fourteen people. That's very high kill to film minute ratio. To redeem that kind of behaviour is no small task. But this is the good news, on actor terms, I mean. He has a physical impairment. A club foot… And then there's his mother. You grimaced. You did. You grimaced. Something about the club foot? The mother? What?

WILLIE: Maybe I could just take the script away for a day or two. Give it a read.

ROSS: Doubts? Pressing doubts? What about. The foot?

The fourteen kills? What? The mother thing?

WILLIE: I just think I should take a look at the script.

ROSS: I wrote the script. I'm the writer-director. Did you know that.

WILLIE: No, I didn't.

ROSS: Someone should have told you. I know you're not insulting the script. You haven't even read it. I'm not that sensitive. But you did grimace.

WILLIE: I didn't mean to grimace. Honestly.

ROSS: Okay. Okay. The part is yours. I want you to do it.

WILLIE: I don't... I mean—

ROSS: It's yours. You're Jonathan. You've got the part.

WILLIE: Yeah?

ROSS: So? Great? Is that...great? Are you—

WILLIE: Yeah but can I—

ROSS: No.

WILLIE: Yeah, but I'd like to—

ROSS: No. No way.

WILLIE: Whatya mean no? I haven't said—

ROSS: You can't read the script! You gotta trust me. I'm trusting you. You didn't even audition. It's a gut thing. Strictly instinct. Whatya say?

WILLIE: I'm sorry but—

ROSS: You can't read the goddamn script! Okay?! You got that?! I'm not letting you read my script, man. Come on. It's only the second draft. You can read it when you show up on the set and not a minute sooner! Okay?! So are you Jonathan the serial killer or not?! Come on. Be a man. Make a decision!

WILLIE: (Sighs.)

ROSS: You sighed. What's that mean? That sigh. Does that mean yes or no. Come on. I haven't got all day.

WILLIE: *(Sighs.)*

ROSS: What!?

               (Music:)

Scene Seven

               (Apartment. WILLIE & Sound: WILLIE is flipping pages. Mumbling, sighing, groaning. Sound: Door opens/closes.)

JESS &
SANDY: *(Come on. Drunk.)*

SANDY: *(Moving on.)* Hi, it's me. I brought Jess.

JESS: *(Moving on.)* We came to apologize. Nice apartment Willie.

SANDY: She came to apologize. I came to get laid.

JESS: Listen, I have to throw up. Where should I do that.

WILLIE: The toilet would be nice.

JESS: Thanks. *(She starts off. Stops.)* Oh. I'm sorry for attacking you before. You just…pissed me off.

WILLIE: You pissed me off too.

JESS: Yeah but I attacked you…physically. That's… unacceptable behaviour. Even for me…I'm sorry. Okay?

WILLIE: Sure.

JESS: Great… *(Moving off.)* I gotta go throw up now.

SANDY: Whatcha readin', Willie.

               (Sound: Door closes.)

WILLIE: Script.

SANDY: That's nice. *(Sits next to him.)* Take your clothes off.
            No, take my clothes off first. You're gonna have to
            take all the clothes off, Willie. Yours and mine. It's
            up to you Willie. I'm drunk. Get to it, boy. No. First
            kiss me.

            (Biz: She grabs him. Kisses him.)

            Okay. Take my sweater off. Here. Take the bottom
            and just pull it over my head. No. First touch my
            breast. Nice… Okay. Take my sweater off now.

WILLIE: Look, can we do this later.

SANDY: Sure. But can we do it now too.

WILLIE: Jess is here.

SANDY: You wanna do it with her?

WILLIE: Come on, sober up a bit. Go make yourself a coffee.

SANDY: I need to be touched.

WILLIE: I'll touch you later. I've got to finish reading this
            thing. *(Pages flip.)* I told the director I'd let him
            know by tomorrow.

SANDY: I don't know, Willie. I thought you were
            spontaneous. You seem to be letting me down here.

WILLIE: It's a job, Sandy. I need the money.

SANDY: I do commercials for money.

WILLIE: I know.

SANDY: I know you know. All I'm saying is. Don't be
            embarrassed. We've all got to make a living. Can I
            give you some advice here. Do it. For the money.
            Whatever it is. What is it… Let me see it.

WILLIE: No.

SANDY: Come on. Let me—

WILLIE: No.

(Biz: A scuffle, pages.)

SANDY: Thanks. Ah not this piece of shit. Okay, look before we go any farther. Don't tell Jess I said it was a piece of shit. I made a big deal about not calling it a piece of shit. I was trying to calm her down. I don't know why. But I feel I should try to calm her down about—

WILLIE: You've read this?

SANDY: I told you I was going to audition. Why don't you ever listen to me.

WILLIE: I don't know.

SANDY: I read for the hooker who gets killed.

WILLIE: Which one. There's fourteen of them.

SANDY: Oh, right, yeah. Ah geez. Sick awful stuff. Okay touch my breast. Put your head somewhere interesting. Do something spontaneous with my body. *(She is snuggling.)*

WILLIE: So did you get the part.

SANDY: No. I wanted to do it as a comedy.

WILLIE: Why.

SANDY: I don't know. To give it some value. I don't know. Hey wait a minute. You can't be in that movie. What's wrong with you. You've got a…you know, reputation. Some of us look up to you.

WILLIE: The money is great.

SANDY: Yeah? Hey wait a minute. What part are you up for.

WILLIE: Jonathan.

SANDY: The killer.

WILLIE: Yeah.

SANDY: Ooooh. Get away from me. You're kidding. Get away. You had your hands on me and all the while you're thinking about playing Jonathan the serial killer. Oooh.

(Sound: Door opens. Closes.)

JESS: *(Moving on.)* I threw up. I had a fast shower. I borrowed your bathrobe, Willie. I borrowed your toothbrush too. I feel better.

SANDY: He's going to be in that stupid movie.

JESS: Which one.

SANDY: He's going to play Jonathan the serial killer.

JESS: *(To WILLIE.)* You shit! *(Slaps him across the back of the head.)*

WILLIE: Hey! You hit me!

JESS: I'm sorry. It was an accident. *(Slaps him across the back of the head again.)*

WILLIE: Hey, knock it off.

JESS: Relax. I told you it was an accident.

SANDY: He had his hands all over me and he was thinking about Jonathan at the same time.

JESS: That's disgusting... Got anything to drink around here, Willie?

WILLIE: Coffee. *(Moves off.)* All I'm serving you two is coffee.

(Sound: Goes to kitchen. Kettle filled, coffee made under:)

SANDY: I wanted him to make love to me. But all he'd do was put his hands on me. That's what Jonathan does. Looks at his victims. Puts his hands on them. And then...out comes the machete.

JESS: *(Shouting to WILLIE.)* Were you in character, Willie. Were you Jonathan. Will you *be* Jonathan, Willie. Make a bundle to kill women on the big screen. Ah Willie I knew you were full of shit!

WILLIE: *(Shouting from kitchen.)* I haven't made any real money in three years!!

SANDY: I make commercials for money. But I've never killed anyone.

JESS: I don't do anything for money.

SANDY: You're an artist.

JESS: Yeah. I am. But I'm not happy about it.

SANDY: Ah. I was really looking forward to getting laid. I don't…much.

JESS: Why not. Are you fussy.

SANDY: Not particularly.

JESS: Well, then I don't understand it. You're beautiful. You should get laid all the time. Willie should have laid you.

SANDY: He had his script.

JESS: He should have put it down. He should have taken you on the couch. I would have.

SANDY: Hey, are you a dyke.

JESS: Smile when you say that.

SANDY: *(Giggles.)* Hey, are you a dyke.

JESS: You've got a nice smile.

SANDY: I've always wanted a dyke as a friend. Oh, this is great. Okay, listen, my feelings about this are pretty complex. I think we should become very close in a spiritual way. Very unguarded and open. But you have to adore me, and want me physically very much. And I have to wrestle with those two major aspects of our friendship. I have to be torn between the spiritual openness and a potential for a new erotic experience. Eventually I can become obsessed with it. It's exactly the kind of thing I need to fill up my life. Okay, so are we going to do that.

JESS: What is it I have to do again.

SANDY: Adore me?

JESS: Yeah right. So do you get to adore me.

SANDY: I wrestle with that. That's another thing I wrestle with. I wrestle with you adoring me and the possibility that I adore you. You know…want you. And how that could affect our open unguarded friendship.

JESS: You're pretty complicated for a blonde.

SANDY: Yeah. You thought I was an idiot. So when you're working and you have to kiss a man do you ever feel anything? What do you feel. Do you think about a woman to make yourself feel something.

JESS: I see we're gonna jump right into this openness thing.

SANDY: So no one in the business knows right. I mean I've never heard them talk about you. So you're, what, in the closet, sort of. Or do you have another life outside the "business". Do you go to those bars. What are they like? Do you dance? I've heard they're fun, those bars. There's a lot of dancing.

JESS: Do you like to dance.

SANDY: Okay, is that a loaded question. Or are you just really asking me if I like to dance.

JESS: Do you?

SANDY: Like to dance? Yeah.

JESS: Okay we'll go.

SANDY: Go where? To one of those bars? Yeah? Wow. Hey I just got a little jolt up through my body. I got…you know…excited.

JESS: Maybe we shouldn't talk about this anymore till you sober up.

WILLIE: (Coming on.) Instant. It's all I've got.

SANDY: Ah don't apologize.

WILLIE: I wasn't apologizing. Drink it. Or don't drink it. I
              don't care.

SANDY: *(To JESS.)* He does really.

WILLIE: So…Jess… What's new.

JESS: Huh?

WILLIE: Got any work?

JESS: I can't talk to you about my professional life, Willie.

WILLIE: No? Why not.

JESS: Well, for two reasons really. One, you think I'm a
              selfish actor. And two, you're going to be Jonathan
              the serial killer.

SANDY: Did he call you a selfish actor.

JESS: A selfish bitch actually. But I assumed he was only
              referring to my work since he doesn't know a thing
              about me personally.

WILLIE: I didn't mean it.

JESS: Sure you did.

WILLIE: I was just trying to make a point. Good actors give
              something to get something. They share.

JESS: Share is a code word, Willie. The actor in me does
              not in any way understand the word "share". I'm
              never hired to share. I'm hired to make a character
              come to life. Any way I can. Look, I don't want to
              talk about acting. It isn't worth the effort.

WILLIE: Yes it is.

JESS: No it's not. It's bullshit.

WILLIE: No, it's not bullshit.

JESS: Can I have some more coffee.

WILLIE: No.

JESS: Why not.

WILLIE: Because you're wrong.

JESS: No, I'm not wrong.

SANDY: And even if she is wrong, that's no reason not to give her more coffee. You're being small.

WILLIE: She just told me the thing I do with my life isn't even worth discussing. That's depressing.

SANDY: So get depressed. That's okay. Just don't get small. You know, petty. It's such an actor thing to do.

WILLIE: Jesus.

JESS: I want to be an engineer. I think I'm going to go back to school and become a structural engineer.

SANDY: Me too... What is a structural engineer. I mean...exactly.

WILLIE: Acting is my life... I can't help it. I have to take it seriously. Do you understand?

JESS: Why do you care if I understand.

WILLIE: I don't care. Not really. It was just an expression. The hell with you for dismissing my life like that.

JESS: Hey calm down. You're getting pathetic.

WILLIE: Jesus! It's my life!

JESS: Hey, get ahold of yourself. I don't know where you get off being so precious about it anyway. You're about to portray Jonathan the serial killer for no other reason than to make a lot of money. You're slime. Really you're worse than slime. You're vomit. I mean professionally speaking. You're a stinking hypocrite and a possible danger to our society.

WILLIE: Ah, drop dead.

SANDY: Maybe we should all have a drink. (*Moving off to kitchen.*) I know where he keeps the liquor.

JESS: I'm starting to feel really hostile towards you again Willie. I've tried to be nice to you, seeing that this is your apartment and everything. But listening to you whine about your life and knowing about your hypocritical determination to bring Jonathan to the big screen, all I want to do is knock your goddamn teeth out.

WILLIE: Listen, okay? Can't you see I'm conflicted here. Can't you see I'm torn.

JESS: Can't you see I don't care.

WILLIE: Right! Because you're a selfish bitch.

JESS: Ooh, there it is again. Okay. You're gonna have to pay for that, Willie.

SANDY: *(Moving on.)* He's got scotch, gin, and vodka. He's got a cheap brandy. Three bottles of red wine. Six imported beers from Brussels. And a bottle of Tia Maria. Whatya want?

JESS: I don't care.

WILLIE: Bring it all.

JESS: Bring it all. Yeah.

SANDY: Yeah. So? ...We're gonna get really hammered. And then what. Sex? *(Pause. Moving off.)* Just a suggestion.

JESS: Okay, Willie. Up you get. Let's duke it out. Let's get to it. Come on, boy. Up.

WILLIE: I have no intention of having a fist fight with you, Jess. Why do you want to beat up on me. Why? I mean it's strange don't you think. You've got a really strong need to punch and kick me. Why. I'd like to know.

JESS: Me too...

WILLIE: Is it because I'm a man.

JESS: Yeah. Maybe. Or maybe it's because you're a pathetic hypocrite who keeps calling me nasty names.

(*Biz: She smacks him across the head.*)

WILLIE: Ouch. Knock it off. (*She does it again.*) I said knock it off.

JESS: Stand up and fight. Come on!

WILLIE: Jesus.

JESS: On your feet Jonathan. Let's see how you do without your machete. Come on Jonathan.

(*Biz: She whacks him.*)

WILLIE: Ouch. Knock it off. Get the hell away from me. And stop calling me Jonathan.

JESS: (*Is moving, breathing heavily.*) You're dead meat, Jonathan. This one's for those fourteen hookers you're gonna kill.

(*Biz: Whacking sound. And another.*)

WILLIE: Ahhh. (*He falls.*) Look at yourself. You're outta control.

JESS: Come on! It's payback time. Ah, Jonathan, you're on your knees. What's wrong. Can't take a fair fight.

WILLIE: I think you broke my nose.

JESS: Good.

WILLIE: It's time to stop. My nose is—

JESS: Not yet. First a little kick in the stomach.

(*Biz: A loud whomping sound. WILLIE groans.*)

He's down. He's down for the count. He's down and out. He's down and gone! Goodbye Jonathan you sicko and all the sicko things you stand for.

(*Sound: SANDY enters carrying several clanging bottles.*)

SANDY: (*Moving on.*) It's a party!

JESS: Count me in.

WILLIE: *(Groans.)*

Scene Eight

> *(Hospital cafeteria. Sound: Fellow lunchers in background. Two trays laid on a table. Two people sit. Some eating and cutlery through scene.)*

WILLIE: Never had a business meeting in a place like this.

ROSS: No? I eat here all the time. I love it. So when you called me from the emergency room, it seemed like...destiny or something. How'd you break your nose anyway.

WILLIE: I don't want to talk about it.

ROSS: Good... There's something dynamic about a hospital cafeteria. A faint echo of the life and death struggle... I take meetings here all the time. Besides, I like the food.

WILLIE: You do?

ROSS: Yeah. It's one of the few places left where you can get liver. Liver...and onions. Steak and kidney pie. Things like that.

WILLIE: Organ food.

ROSS: High in iron. And protein of course. And you get big servings. Look how much I've got on my plate. Also I like the desserts. Butterscotch. One of the few places left where you can get butterscotch things. Things from my childhood. I'm into my childhood in a major way. Everything I do, I do because of my childhood.

WILLIE: Is that bad or good.

ROSS: Whatya mean?

WILLIE: Well, did you have a good childhood and you're just trying to relive it...or did you have a rotten childhood that totally stunted your emotional growth.

ROSS: What are you saying. Is this about my script. Was
                 that a comment directed at my writing.

WILLIE: No…not really. No. I—

ROSS: I'm a basic guy. I just like basic things. I thought
                 you liked my script. You sounded like you liked it
                 on the phone. Otherwise why are we meeting.

WILLIE: I'm interested in the character.

ROSS: He's fascinating, isn't he. Jonathan. He's like
                 our…worst fear. Isn't he? But also he's appealing in
                 a strange way. Isn't he.

WILLIE: I'm interested in the character. But I don't think he's
                 appealing in any way at all.

ROSS: You don't think he appeals to some deep-seated
                 male thing.

WILLIE: What deep-seated male thing are you talking
                 about?

ROSS: The deep-seated male…thing…that doesn't really
                 like women.

WILLIE: You think that exists?

ROSS: You don't?

WILLIE: In all men? No.

ROSS: But in some men…

WILLIE: Sure. Men like Jonathan. Deranged terrified evil
                 sick men.

ROSS: But not in anyone else?

WILLIE: You mean you?

ROSS: Me?

WILLIE: You don't like women?

ROSS: I like women as much as any man likes women.

WILLIE: How. How do you like them.

ROSS:	Is this about Jonathan. Shouldn't we just talk about Jonathan.
WILLIE:	Okay. Look, the thing is I have to know what you're trying to do with this character. Are you just screwing around. Just going for a big sick thrill. Is that what you think you're doing. Putting a big awful sick thing out in front of the audience and seeing how much you can scare them.
ROSS:	Scaring them is okay. It's a legitimate thing to do. It's a, you know…a genre. The horror genre.
WILLIE:	Right. But also… Well, are you working on some personal demons here. Is Jonathan your alter ego? Your movie persona… You know what I mean?
ROSS:	Jesus. I know what you mean. But Jesus. Jonathan isn't me. He's…Jonathan. And really if he's a demon…he's everyone's…
WILLIE:	No. That's wrong. I already told you I don't believe that.
ROSS:	Maybe you're hiding something from yourself. Maybe you've got the deep-seated thing too.
WILLIE:	I don't.
ROSS:	I say maybe you do.
WILLIE:	But…I don't.
ROSS:	Look. I'm the writer. You're just an actor. No offence, but you'd have to give me the benefit of any doubt about this.
WILLIE:	Like hell I would. You're talking about my subconscious. I guess I'd know more about that than any frigging screenwriter.
ROSS:	Then how do you explain all the great film classics?
WILLIE:	What?
ROSS:	The great film classics were all written by someone who knew more about people than any psychiatrist

or anyone else. That's why they're, you know...timeless.

WILLIE: Look we're moving off subject here.

ROSS: No, I don't think so. You just don't understand the process. Only writers understand the process.

WILLIE: What process.

ROSS: The writing process...

WILLIE: What's that have to do with—

ROSS: Jonathan is part of the process. It's a timeless process. It's part public, part private. You think I'm Jonathan because Jonathan is brilliantly written, and that must mean I'm Jonathan because how else could I have written him so...you know...brilliantly.

WILLIE: I don't want to do anything that just helps you get your rocks off.

ROSS: Look, I know what your problem is. You want this part very badly. But it's a stretch. You're scared of it...

WILLIE: Ah Jesus.

ROSS: It's an actor thing. I've seen it before. You're scared of failing so you're looking for a way out.

WILLIE: That's garbage. What do you know about actors. I just have some legitimate questions about—

ROSS: Look, there's a lot of money in this for you. So even if you fail you'll have the money. So why not just take the job and all the money that goes with it and keep your questions to yourself.

WILLIE: I...ah...can't.

ROSS: So what do you want from me... Okay, he's a killer. He's a psycho. He kills women. He's very nasty. I hate him. I hate his guts. I never want to be anything like him.

WILLIE: So kill him.

ROSS: What.

WILLIE: You've got to kill him off. He's got to die. Right now he escapes. He just disappears. That's not good.

ROSS: I can't have him killed.

WILLIE: Why not?

ROSS: Jesus. Actors, man. Are they naive or what. Because of the sequel.

WILLIE: Get serious. You think there's gonna be a demand for more of this crap.

ROSS: Okay I won't take that personally. Just to show you I'm a professional I'll let that hurtful remark pass… Anyway I've already signed for the sequel so fuck you.

WILLIE: You mean I'd have to do him twice?

ROSS: At least. We're talking about options on three more.

WILLIE: Jesus. That makes five… Five!

ROSS: At least. Okay. Look. He can't die. But he can be captured in a very violent way. And then escape. It'll be a recurring, you know, "motif".

WILLIE: Jesus.

ROSS: What's wrong with you? You're turning very pale.

WILLIE: I'll be Jonathan the rest of my life.

ROSS: You'll be rich. What's wrong with that. Take the part. Get rich. This is the kind of advice your agent should be giving you.

WILLIE: My agent believes in me. In my judgment.

ROSS: Your agent thinks you're a stage actor with limited commercial potential. So she doesn't give a shit what you do. When I call her and tell her about the sequels she'll be all over you to take the part.

WILLIE: I could just walk away…

ROSS: You're Jonathan. I had a dream about him. He looked like you. I need you to be in my movie. It'll make you rich and famous. Screw all the other stuff. That's for critics and social workers. I gotta make this thing. And I need an actor. And that actor is you.

WILLIE: You're buying me.

ROSS: Yeah. Good. Think of it that way. That's easier. I'm buying you. It's not about anything in your psyche or my psyche or anything sociological or anything about your talent and what you should be doing with it… You're being bought…and really there's nothing you can do about it… Because you're being bought with an enormous amount of money.

WILLIE: Yeah but—

ROSS: Now just shut the hell up and let me finish my lunch in peace… God this was a nerve-wracking experience. If I hadn't dreamed about you as Jonathan I'd have shot right outta here… You were getting at some very uncomfortable places in me. My writing. My taste. My childhood. My manness. Good thing I like actors.

WILLIE: (Sighs.)

ROSS: There's that sigh again. What's that mean. Do you give in? Is that a sigh of resignation. Is this a deal or what.

WILLIE: I… I'll think about it.

ROSS: Good… In the meantime, wanna try this liver?

WILLIE: (Weakly.) No.

ROSS: Come on. It's good. Come on. Open up… Come on. Look, I'll give you fifty bucks if you'll take a bite. Really. Fifty bucks hard cash. Okay a hundred. Don't tell me you don't need it. Come on a hundred bucks just to try a little piece of liver. Hey, it was just a joke… Come on. Try it anyway. Try it for free... Okay fuck you. *(He laughs.)* I mean that with affection. *(Laughs.)*

WILLIE: *(Sighs.)*

Scene Nine

(WILLIE's apartment. JESS and SANDY asleep on pullout couch. Breathing peacefully. Sound: Door closes. WILLIE comes in. Walks over to:)

WILLIE: *(Whispering.)* Sandy... Sandy are you asleep. I need to talk.

SANDY: Hmm.

WILLIE: Wake up. *(He nudges her.)* Wake up, okay.

            (Sound: Sheets rustle.)

SANDY: Hmm. *(She stirs.)* Ah... What... Hmmm. Hi.

WILLIE: Hi... Sorry to wake you but...

JESS: *(Groans.)*

SANDY: Lower your voice. You'll wake up Jess.

WILLIE: Jess? Is that Jess under the covers.

SANDY: Yeah. Who'd you think it was.

WILLIE: I didn't— Why are you both sleeping here?

SANDY: Where should we be sleeping. Why do you have this pull-out couch if you don't want people sleeping on it. Where you been. You've been out all night.

WILLIE: I went for a walk. I had to think. About my life. It just seemed like the thing to do. Walk and think about my life. Then I went to the hospital to get my nose looked at. It's broken. Then I had a lunch meeting with that director.

SANDY: Lunch? What time is it.

WILLIE: I dunno. Early afternoon. I need to talk.

SANDY: Sure.

WILLIE: He's nuts. That director guy. He's a lunatic. How he gets money to make a film, I don't know... I just don't get it. Because he's nuts and he's... Are you naked under that cover.

SANDY: Yeah.

WILLIE: Oh... Is Jess naked too.

SANDY: Yeah...

WILLIE: Really...

SANDY: I discovered something about myself last night Willie. Something interesting. I'm a bisexual.

WILLIE: Really.

SANDY: Yeah. Who would have thought. Not me.

WILLIE: Me either.

SANDY   I know what you're thinking. You're thinking it was just the liquor. But it wasn't. I'm bisexual by nature. It's wonderful. It's just opened up a whole new world of possibilities. I'm excited by that. You're my friend Willie so I want you to be excited for me too. Are you.

WILLIE: I'm thrilled.

SANDY: No. You're threatened.

WILLIE: I'm not threatened.

SANDY: Well, then you're confused.

WILLIE: No, I'm not confused.

SANDY: Please don't be dishonest. It just proves that you're confused and threatened.

WILLIE: Okay. Look. I don't think I'm threatened but maybe I'm a bit confused. It's kind of a surprise. Truth is

I'm not sure how I feel about it. I'm not sure how I feel about you. I mean I thought we had… Look. I can't deal with this now anyway. I've got a major career decision to make. I can't think about you right now. I can only think about me. I was hoping you'd help me.

SANDY: Help you what? Think about yourself?

WILLIE: Yeah.

SANDY: Well, I guess I could do that. But… I just thought you'd be happy for me. Or at least interested. I made love to a woman last night. That's kind of a big deal. Don't you think.

WILLIE: Maybe. But I've got to make a decision that's going to affect the rest of my life. That's a bigger deal. What about Jess.

SANDY: What about her.

WILLIE: I mean did you both decide you were bisexual at the same time or—

SANDY: She's gay.

WILLIE: Oh. Well, that explains a lot.

SANDY: What does it explain.

WILLIE: A lot. Look. I can't talk about this now. I've got to tell this lunatic whether I'm doing his movie or not. And I've got to tell him today. So whatya think.

SANDY: I can't think about that after what you said about Jess.

WILLIE: What did I say.

SANDY: When I told you she was gay, you said that explained a lot.

WILLIE: I don't want to talk about Jess. I want to talk about me.

SANDY: Well, I want to talk about Jess. And I want to talk about your attitude towards Jess. And I want to talk about what happened between me and Jess. But, you know what. What I want to talk about most is me. That's right. I do. I want to talk about me.

WILLIE: Sure. Okay. But me first.

SANDY: Why you first? Me first. Then you.

WILLIE: There's plenty of time for you—

SANDY: That's what you always say. But I think the time for me is now. That's my new slogan. The time for me is now. What do you think of it.

WILLIE: I don't think anything about it. Because I'm thinking about myself.

SANDY: The time for me is now. I love it. You know why?

(And they both talk at once.)

SANDY:
Because I feel I've entered a new phase. Some different thing from who I was. Because who I was was someone who did the same thing I'd done for a long time. Things I was expected to do. Being an actor. Looking the way I look. Doing Toyota commercials. Going to see better actors doing serious plays and not having the courage to say no to Toyota commercials. Because I was expected to be a certain way. Not too serious or courageous. But now that I'm different in one way at least I feel I could be different in a lot of ways. So this is the beginning of that... So now it's time for me to be whatever I am, and whatever I could be because, well, you know...

WILLIE:
Look. By 3 or 4 o'clock I could be signing a piece of paper that changes my life. Takes me out of this world and into a new world. A world of money and power. I've got a feeling if I do this movie it's going to propel me somewhere. This sicko director and his sicko killer Jonathan are going to change my life. It's like a pact with the devil I'm about to sign. I was born to be a serious actor. I've given a lot of time to my profession, tried to pass along a certain philosophy, done my best to instill respect and dignity in my students and my colleagues. But I'm not a kid. I've got nothing. No pension. Nothing. And this part in this sicko movie will change that. All I've got to do is come to terms with denying my entire life up to this point. I mean... What should I, you know...do?

(Pause.)

WILLIE: Well?

SANDY: Well what? That's about it.

WILLIE: What do you think about what I just said?

SANDY: You said something?

WILLIE: Weren't you listening?

SANDY: Weren't you.

WILLIE: Ah. You're still drunk. I'm not gonna waste any more of my time talking to a drunk... *(Moving off.)* I've gotta do some work with this script.

SANDY: You going somewhere? I might have more to say.

WILLIE: *(Off.)* I'll be in the bathroom. Did you just ask me a question?

         (Sound: Bathroom door closes.)

SANDY: *(Shouting.)* No! Did you ask me one!

WILLIE: *(Shouting through door.)* No!

SANDY: Prick! Oh hi, Jess you're awake.

         (Sound: Sheets rustle.)

JESS: *(Sighs. A bit groggy.)* Yeah. Amazing, eh.

SANDY: Sorry. I forgot you were here. I just had some stuff to get off my chest.

JESS: Yeah.

SANDY: Did you hear my new motto?

JESS: "The time for you is now"?

SANDY: Yeah. What do you think about it?

JESS: I think you need therapy.

SANDY: Why?

JESS: Whatya mean, "why"? You should listen to
             yourself.

SANDY: My problem isn't me listening to me. It's getting
             anyone else to listen to me.

JESS: Well, who wants to listen to you when all you talk
             about is your frigging Toyota commercial.

ROSS: *(Off.)* Hello... Hello. The door was open... So I just
             came in.

SANDY: The door was open?

ROSS: *(Coming on.)* I mean unlocked. It wasn't locked. So
             I...just came in.

SANDY: You looking for Willie?

ROSS: Yeah... I'm—

SANDY: I know who you are.

ROSS: You do? We've met or something?

SANDY: Yesterday. At the audition.

ROSS: Really? Oh...oh yeah...you're...you're...ah...ah...

SANDY: Sandy.

ROSS: Right. Sandy.

SANDY: This is Jess. You met her yesterday too.

ROSS: Oh...right. So how are you. Am I disturbing you...
             Hey, I remember you now. You're two of the sluts I
             saw.

JESS: Is it possible if given the chance you'd like to
             rephrase that, slimeball.

ROSS: I didn't mean sluts. I meant hookers. You
             know...the parts...in the script. I mean the—
             Slimeball? Did you call me slimeball?

JESS: You have a problem with that? You're saying no
             one's ever called you a slimeball before?

ROSS: Hey, I remember you now. You're the hooker who walked out. And you. You're the other hooker who walked out.

SANDY: You can't say "You're the hooker who walked out." You have to say, "You're the actor who walked out." Anyway I didn't walk out. I just refused to read.

ROSS: Yeah right. Refused to read because I wouldn't let you make it funny. Wow. So you're a pair, eh. The two of you are…like…together. Okay okay, now it makes sense.

JESS: (To SANDY, in a whisper.) This is gonna get ugly. Are you ready?

SANDY: I think so.

JESS: (To ROSS.) What makes sense, slimeball. Do you mean you have some new understanding of why we had trouble associating ourselves with that adolescent piece of crap that came out of your sad uninformed little weasel brain. You think because the two of us have shared some pleasure we're somehow incapable of appreciating that rancid sewage you're about to turn into a movie for dangerously aggressive adolescent wankers.

ROSS: Look I just came here to see Willie about the part I want him to do. I had nothing else on my mind. But you're here. You're calling me a slimeball. I'm remembering the aggravating shit you put me through yesterday and it's not like I don't have an ego or anything. Or feelings or anything. It's not like a couple of sweethearts like you can put me through that kind of irritating new age feminist neurotic unprofessional bullshit and I'm not gonna have a response. Because I do. I've got a response. And this is it. Fuck you!! You uptight little dyke. Fuck you!

JESS: (Groans loudly.)

SANDY: I'm afraid we're going to have to ask you to leave now.

ROSS: Tough. I came here to see Willie, and I'm staying till
             I do. And you wanna know something else? I did
             mean to say sluts. Sluts is the word I meant all
             along.

JESS: *(To SANDY.)* I feel at a disadvantage here. We have
             to get up. Words aren't enough for this slimeball.
             He needs a little bodily contact.

SANDY: We're naked under this thing.

JESS: We'll get dressed. He'll wait. Won't you slimeball.

ROSS: I'm not going anywhere till I see Willie. I'm not
             afraid of you.

JESS: We'll see. *(Starts to get up, sheets rustle.)*

SANDY: *(Grabbing her.)* We can't show this guy our bodies.
             This is the guy who invented Jonathan. You want
             him dreaming about us?

JESS: Turn your back, slimeball. And keep your eyes
             closed.

ROSS: No problem… *(Turns off.)* Happy now?

JESS: And no peeking. We don't want your eyes on our
             exposed flesh for even a fraction of a second.

             (Sound: Sheets rustle as they get out of bed.)

ROSS: Weirdos. You're just weirdo actors. I've seen
             dozens of them. And you're right in there with the
             weirdest.

JESS: Get our clothes.

SANDY: They're all over the floor. Here, these are yours.

JESS: No, those are yours. These are mine.

             (Biz: They are grabbing clothes, getting dressed.)

ROSS: It's like you're living in some other world. The stuff
             you've got on your minds. It's not human. You
             wanna know something? You wanna know why
             my movie is gonna be big? Because it's human. It's

ugly, but it's human. It's in touch with human ugliness. And that's big. Human ugliness is big.

SANDY: Got everything?

JESS: Enough for now.

SANDY: Leave the shoes.

JESS: Okay. *(Moving off.)* Let's go to the bathroom.

SANDY: Willie's there… *(Moving off.)* Head for the kitchen.

                (Biz: They are hobbling off.)

JESS: We'll be back, slimeball—don't go anywhere. You and I are gonna get it on.

ROSS: I'll be here. Right here!

                (Biz: SANDY and JESS in kitchen. We can hear them moving around, getting dressed under:)

Standing right on this spot. Waiting. Standing and waiting right here right where I fucking am! With this… My script. *(He bangs it.)* Right here. Standing proud. Because I'm not some weirdo actor from another world. I'm from this world right here. And that's why I'm gonna be big. Because I'm in touch with where I am… Hey! And if I wanna call you a slut, I will. Because I'm big enough to call you a slut and you're just a nothing little neurotic and I can squash you like a bug. And you know what else I can do to you? I can buy you. When you come outta that kitchen I can look you in the eye and name a figure and you'll be bought. You'll cease to exist as a separate entity and you'll be lousy chattel. The right amount of cash dollars and you'll even forget your name and everything you thought you believed in. And if I give you enough money and I tell you to look that way or this way or some other way you'll fucking do it. And if I tell you to say something you'll say it. If I tell you to say you love my screenplay you'll say, "I love your screenplay." And if I tell you to be in my movie and play a scene with Jonathan and be his victim you'll do it. And then you'll do publicity for the movie. And you'll say wonderful things about me, including things like, "He's a great man, a courageous genius. He's definitely in touch with the real world in which we live and I'm proud to be associated with him! I worship the ground he walks on. I lick the pavement beneath his shoes. I'm nothing. He's everything. I'm just an actor. He's a creator. I'm a bug. He's a god! Yes! When you consider all that he's had to endure to put his vision on the big screen, all the niggling politically correct crap he's had to endure from buglike-neo-fascistic bitter little know-nothing scummy bugs like me the only thing you can say about him is that he's a god!"

JESS: *(A loud sustained scream as she comes running on and attacks ROSS.)*

(Sound: Things being knocked over.)

Hey God. It's me. The bug. Make me an offer!

(Sound: Body hitting the floor.)

ROSS: Hey, get off me. Get away. Ouch! Hey stop! Hey, man. You're kicking me… Hey! Ow…

JESS: Make me an offer. Come on, make me an offer.

(Biz: She kicks him.)

ROSS: Argghhhh! Fifty thousand.

(Biz: She kicks him again.)

SANDY: *(Rushing out.)* Jess. Don't.

JESS: I gotta.

(Biz: Kicks him again.)

ROSS: Oww. Hundred thousand. Plus points. No buyout. Piece of the video sale.

JESS: Fuck off. And die!

(Biz: Kicks him. SANDY goes over. Tries to pull JESS off. Sounds of a scuffle.)

HOW TO MAKE LOVE TO AN ACTOR

SANDY: You're hurting him.

JESS: Good. Let me go, Sandy. Let me at him.

ROSS: Okay, okay, we're gonna get serious. Two hundred thousand. Ouch. You play the first hooker. You get billing. You get two hundred grand but...fuck you you're gonna die just like the rest of them.

JESS: In your dreams, asshole!

            (Music: Sudden music. Strange and dissonant. An animal-like growl. It grows.)

SANDY: The light... What's happening.

            (The animal growling gets closer.)

JESS: It's Willie.

SANDY: Willie... Willie what are you—

ROSS: It's not Willie. It's Jonathan.

JESS: Ah...shit.

ROSS: Look at him. He's...beautiful.

WILLIE: *(Starts to move around, slowly. One foot dragging. When he speaks he has a new voice, full of menace.)* Look at me. I want you to look at me. Tell me I'm...beautiful. Don't you think I'm beautiful. Don't you want to get close to me. Rub up against my body. Have my beauty all around you. Get crushed by my beauty. Have my beauty inside you. *(He continues to shuffle around.)*

JESS: Jesus...

ROSS: It's the beauty speech... Scene...scene number... Where's my script? I dropped it. Oh. There.

            (Sound: Script picked up. Pages flipped.)

WILLIE: I am a thing of nature. A thing of beauty. Do you want a beautiful thing of nature inside you.

ROSS: Scene number 35. Interior. Seedy hotel room. Night. Jonathan comes out of the bathroom. In a lumberjack shirt and panty hose. The hooker looks at him. Laughs... Okay you. Sandy. Here. Read it.

SANDY: Get serious... Willie, are those my panty hose you're wearing.

ROSS: I'll pay you. Five hundred dollars.

SANDY: Okay.

JESS: Hey come on. Are you nuts.

SANDY: She's right. I can't do it. It's disgusting.

ROSS: No, it's the beauty speech. It leads up to the point of redemption. He can't do it alone. He needs a hooker. There's a journey. They go on it together... Look at him. He's gorgeous. I gotta hear the scene. I'll give you a thousand dollars to read it. I've got a thousand in my wallet.

            (Sound: Money from wallet changes hands underneath:)

            Here. Take it. Take it. Good. Okay. Okay. Read. Read. I'm begging you. Look at him. He's into it. He's Jonathan. He's waiting. He gave you the cue. "Do you want a beautiful thing of nature inside you." That's what he says. "Do you want a beautiful thing of nature inside you." ...And you say...and you say...

            (Sound: Script passed to SANDY.)

SANDY: And I get to keep the thousand. Right.

ROSS: Yeah. He says "Do you want a beautiful thing of nature inside you." And you say...

SANDY: *(Reading.)* Ah... What?

WILLIE: I said! ...I said I've got a thing on me. It's beautiful. Do you *want* it.

SANDY: *(Reading.)* What... Oh, sure. Your thing.

WILLIE: *(Moving towards her.)* Answer my question!

SANDY: *(Reading.)* Hey. Calm down, mister.

WILLIE: Do you *want* my beautiful thing. Do you *want* it *inside* you.

SANDY: *(Reading.)* Yes. Yes, I want it.

WILLIE: Why!?

SANDY: *(Reading.)* Why?… Because it's…beautiful?

WILLIE: No! No! No, that's not why you want it. You don't want it because it's beautiful. You don't know anything about beauty. You only *know* about slime. It's the *slime* you want. And it's the slime you're gonna get.

          (Sound: WILLIE draws a butcher knife from his clothes. It clangs on something.)

SANDY: *(Reading.)* What's that!

JESS: *(To ROSS.)* She says "What's that?" He pulls out a knife big enough to cut down a tree and she says "What's that?"

ROSS: Shut up.

JESS: Why? Are we getting close to the point of redemption here.

ROSS: Shut up. I'll give you five thousand dollars if you'll just shut up… *(To SANDY.)* Okay, ah—Sandy. Keep going. "What's that. What's that!"

SANDY: *(Reading.)* What's that!

WILLIE: You know what it is… It's the thing of beauty… And you're gonna have it inside you.

JESS: Okay. That's it. Five thousand can't keep me quiet when I hear this crap. I'm gonna puke. Knock it off, Willie. You say another word, I'm gonna scream, then I'm gonna puke all over you.

WILLIE: *(Growls.)*

ROSS: Hey. Scream. That's a cue. That's a line. You skipped a few. But it's a cue line somewhere.

WILLIE: Scream. I want you to scream. *(Moving towards JESS.)* I want you to scream for the beauty thing.

ROSS: Hit him!

JESS: What? Hey Willie stay away from me.

ROSS: Hit him. No, you...ah Sandy. Hit him. The hooker hits him.

SANDY: She's the hooker. He's doing it with her now.

JESS: He's not doing it with me. I'm not doing anything. I'll hit him though. Willie if you come another step towards me being Jonathan I'll crack your face open!

ROSS: No. She slaps him. Slap him.

JESS: Willie. You hear me? I don't know what you're pulling but you're starting to piss me off.

SANDY: Me too.

ROSS: Slap him. I'll give you five thousand dollars if you slap him. Slap him. Slap him. Slap him. Five thousand dollars. Five thousand. Slap him. Slap him!

JESS: Willie, I'm warning you. Back off.

WILLIE: *(Moving towards JESS.)* Here it comes, slut. The natural thing of beauty.

JESS: Willie, you asshole!

> *(Biz: JESS slaps WILLIE viciously across the face. WILLIE groans. Drops the knife.)*

ROSS: Hey, why'd you drop the knife. He doesn't drop it.

WILLIE: *(Pause.)* That hurt!

ROSS: What? He doesn't say that. He doesn't say "That hurt"... He falls to the floor. Crying. Fall to the floor. And cry... Come on. Like this. Pick up the thing of beauty. Cradle it. Like this.

(ROSS is on the floor. Crying.)

WILLIE: *(Has his own voice back.)* It's a basic thing. A basic goddamn thing you learn in maybe the first year of drama school. You don't actually hit the person you're supposed to hit. *(To JESS.)* I think you might have broken my goddamn jaw. What's wrong with you. I thought you were an actor. I thought you had some training.

JESS: I'm sorry. I got mad.

WILLIE: You were supposed to get mad. That was okay. But you still have to have some control. I thought you knew that.

JESS: I wasn't acting! I hit you because you pissed me off.

WILLIE: Well, who gave you permission to do that.

JESS: I didn't need permission. I wasn't acting. You were acting...I was just pissed off. Get it? Get the difference?

ROSS: Mommy? Mommy? I didn't meant to do it. Why'd you have to go and hurt me like that. Mommy? Mommy? *(Continues to cry.)*

JESS: Mommy? *(To WILLIE.)* He falls to the floor and says "Mommy" like that?

WILLIE: Well, I was probably gonna just crumble on to my knees. Maybe mumble the first two mommies. Maybe mumble the whole speech.

SANDY: You know maybe just mumbling the whole scene would be better. Or just mumble the whole script from beginning to end.

WILLIE: I thought of that...

SANDY: Yeah. Then maybe it'd be okay. I mean if we didn't actually have to hear any of the dialogue.

JESS: Hey! God! Stop crying... You know, you're quite a sick little puppy. Maybe you should seek professional help. Have you ever considered doing that?

ROSS: *(Whimpering.)* He didn't get to the point of redemption...I didn't get to see if it works.

JESS: Trust me. It doesn't. Nothing could redeem this stuff. Nothing! What's he do next, Willie? After all that mommy stuff.

WILLIE: He jumps up suddenly and cuts her throat. Then cuts her into about fifty pieces. And then he has this long speech he delivers to one of her internal organs. It's more stuff about his mother and how she abused him. And he cries and then he howls. And you fade out on an extreme close-up of his howling mouth.

JESS: *(To ROSS.)* And that's your idea of Jonathan's point of redemption, slimeball. You throw in the child abuse stuff, eh. You manipulative little scumsucking eel.

ROSS: Hey, I offered you big money to shut up. All you had to do was keep your big weirdo actor's mouth closed and you'd have five grand. When was the last time you made five grand? Never, I bet. And anyway what the hell do you know about what I'm getting at here. Do you know anything about Jonathan and his mother. No! You don't. Do you know the sources I drew on for this thing? They're classic. Classic sources. Greek! They're Greek! And they're Shakespearean. Big Greek Shakespearean sources not to mention the Catholics. Scorcese and Coppola and Pasolini and all those other great Catholic guys and their sources about mothers and Jonathan prototypes and the classic hate love beauty sex death punishment guilt violence redemption panorama. So to hell with you! I'm outta here... *(He starts off. Stops.)* You know what you can't deal with here? You can't deal with my enthusiasm. I have enthusiasm and that's just chewing up your insides. Hey I'm your worst nightmare!

JESS: You got that right.

ROSS: Yeah. Because I'm enthusiastic. And I've got money and power.

JESS: And a very, very small penis. And a very, very warped view of the world based on a sad belief that your very, very, very small penis makes you a very, very, very, very small man.

ROSS: I have a large penis. I have a damn fine penis. I have the penis of a man in his prime. And anyway I don't call my penis a penis. I call it—

JESS: I bet you call it all sorts of things.

ROSS: One of the things I call it is big. Mr. Big. Because it is. Do you want to see it?

JESS: Yes. Yes I do.

ROSS: Well, I'm not going to show you. Because I don't have to show you. I have nothing to prove to you. You're nothing.

JESS: Yeah. I know. I'm a bug. You're a god. And I'm a bug. With a bug's eyes. Big bug eyes that will see your small penis in all its limp pathetic misery.

ROSS: You'll never make a movie in this town. I'll see to that. I mean I don't even know who you are. I don't even know your name. But I'll find out your name and I'll make sure you'll never get film work in this town. Not even as an extra. Nothing. Ever. I've got that kind of power. It was given to me. I'm going to use it. I'm going to use it to make my movie and to crush bugs like you!

JESS: You have to leave now. If you don't leave you'll be murdered. You see that knife on the floor?

ROSS: Go ahead. Kill me you crazy bitch! I'm willing to die for what I believe in.

SANDY: Here's your thousand dollars back.

                     (Sound: Money handed over.)

ROSS: Keep it. Who cares. I don't need anything from you. *(He pounds his script.)* Because I've got this!! My script. You. What's your name. Jonathan…Willie. We start on the fifteenth. Your agent will get the details. We're outta here. Me and my script. *(Moving off.)* We have walked through the valley of death the valley of the bug people the valley of political correctness and we have feared no evil... *(Leaves muttering to himself.)*

(Sound: Door opens/slams.)

WILLIE: I told you he was a lunatic. I mean someone has given this guy gazillions of dollars to make a movie. How does he get anyone to give him anything except directions to a mental hospital.

JESS: He got you to give him Jonathan. I mean there you are Willie. In your pantyhose. Cradling your thing of beauty.

SANDY: Are those mine? The pantyhose?

WILLIE: Yours wouldn't fit me. I bought them. Bought the knife too. Couldn't find a machete. Spent about a hundred bucks on makeup. Well, I had to see what it felt like. You know...being Jonathan...

JESS: Yeah. So?

WILLIE: Well... You wanna know the truth?

JESS: Why? Are you going to say you liked it.

SANDY: Oh dear.

WILLIE: The truth is, liking it never actually becomes an issue. You just get inside. Find the one thing you can attach yourself to. Believe it. Say the lines. Just like everything else I've done. The same really.

JESS: Really?

WILLIE: Yeah.

SANDY: I think I'd like some coffee.

JESS: So what was it. The one thing...the thing about him you could believe.

WILLIE: I could believe he liked killing women.

JESS: Really… Jesus. You could "attach" yourself to that, eh. You could understand that.

SANDY: So. Does anyone else want any coffee.

WILLIE: I didn't say I could understand it. I could believe it. I didn't *try* to understand it. I just, you know, attached myself to the belief that he really liked doing it.

JESS: And that worked for you.

WILLIE: It felt okay.

SANDY: So. Okay. Good. *(Moving to kitchen.)* I'm gonna make coffee now for all of us.

JESS: Whatya mean it felt okay?

WILLIE: I'm just talking about being inside the character. I was trying to see if I could find a way to actually do the guy.

             (Sound: SANDY making coffee in the kitchen.)

JESS: And you did?

WILLIE: Yeah.

JESS: How?

WILLIE: I just told you how.

JESS: By attaching to his "belief"?

WILLIE: Yeah.

JESS: That's bullshit.

WILLIE: In what way.

JESS: In every way.

WILLIE: You mean as an actor?

JESS: As an actor. As a man. As a human being.

WILLIE: Well, maybe as a man. And a human being. But as an actor it's a legitimate method.

JESS:	How can you have a way of processing things as an actor that wouldn't be suitable for you as a man or a human being.
WILLIE:	That's what acting's all about.
JESS:	What? Doing things you wouldn't actually do?
WILLIE:	Sometimes.
JESS:	Shut up.
WILLIE:	You shut up. I'm just being honest.
JESS:	Being honest? Being honest would be if you just said you wanted the money.
WILLIE:	I've admitted I want the money.
JESS:	And the fame. And the power.
WILLIE:	I could use a little fame and power.
SANDY:	*(Moving on.)* I'm…back.
JESS:	Being honest would be for you to admit you really do understand why Jonathan likes to kill women. Because you do.
WILLIE:	But I don't.
JESS:	Sure you do. Deep down inside you do.
WILLIE:	Ah go to hell.
SANDY:	Coffee will be ready in a minute.
WILLIE:	I just want to know Jess, what makes you think you know what goes on inside me.
JESS:	A feeling.
WILLIE:	Based on what.
JESS:	A feeling.
WILLIE:	A feeling based on a feeling? Shut up.

(Sound: Clang of knife.)

JESS: Here. Here's your knife, your thing of beauty. You dropped it. Here take it. Kill me.

WILLIE: Ah Jesus.

JESS: Look. Why don't you just admit you want to. We're here alone.

SANDY: You're not actually. I mean I'm…here.

JESS: *(To WILLIE.)* Why don't you just get it off your chest. You're sitting there with your thing of beauty. Just admit you want to kill me with it. Cut me up. That deep down, you've got a "belief" that you'd like to kill me. Admit it. Go ahead.

WILLIE: Okay.

JESS: Okay what?

WILLIE: I'd like to kill you.

JESS: I thought so… Why.

WILLIE: Because you're an asshole.

JESS: That's not why.

WILLIE: Believe me. That's why. You're a major asshole.

JESS: Well, I may be an asshole. But that's not why you wanna kill me.

WILLIE: Oh you think I wanna kill you because I've got a small dick or I hate my mother or something. Or because you've had sex with…with…

SANDY: Me. Sex with me.

JESS: Sex is power for you.

WILLIE: Shit. Look having sex with Sandy has nothing to do with anything. Sandy has a good body. People like Sandy's body. I have no problem with that.

SANDY: That's big of you.

JESS: I think you do. I think you've had her to yourself too long. Hanging on your every word. Having her body at your disposal.

SANDY: Come on. I never—

JESS: And now she's infatuated with me. I've got her body now. That's a loss of power. That drives you crazy.

WILLIE: Crazy enough to kill you? Come on.

SANDY: Hey. Nobody has my body…I mean it's still my—

JESS: But there's a way out for you Willie.

SANDY: I thought it was mutual. You know, kind of—

JESS: Stop seeing things from just your own point of view. Stop worrying just about yourself. Think about other people's needs. If you don't you'll turn out just like Jonathan.

WILLIE: Get real.

JESS: Jonathan's afraid of things. Things he's not. Women, for example. You've got to put yourself in a woman's shoes.

WILLIE: Yours?

JESS: Why not. I've got problems too. I'm scared.

WILLIE: Sure you're scared. We're all scared. But right now I've got to make the scariest decision an actor ever has to make. And you're not helping me by going on about—

SANDY: I've made *love* to both you people. You didn't *have* my body—

JESS: The scariest thing an actor has to do is to decide to become an actor. Especially if you're a woman.

WILLIE: No, that's just—

SANDY: If I can't trust you with my body, who can I trust.

JESS: To decide to give yourself up to a world where other people make decisions for you. Based on some pretty dubious values…

WILLIE: You see, if I do this movie I'll lose control of—

JESS: To lose control of your destiny. Your dignity.

SANDY: Not to mention feelings. I gave myself to you both because it meant something.

WILLIE: I've given myself to my profession.

JESS: I've tried to be true to myself, my sex, my beliefs but…

(And they proceed simultaneously.)

JESS:
You know I could just quit. I think about quitting all the time. What's to keep me in this crappy business. There's no real simple truth to be found here. I can't ever be myself. I have to pretend I'm someone weaker and more mainstream. And that's not even taking the emotional toll into account. What happens when you have to sit on your fears and anxieties. Have to deny the knowledge you have that they're out to get you. And if they found out who you really are. How strong you really were they'd want to destroy you… just… destroy you.

WILLIE:
So instead of doing a number on my head based on some agenda you have about sex bias and gender warfare maybe you culd just try to understand how hard it is for me, a man of my age and reputation and how much I've got at stake. I mean this is the thing. Okay? I mean there's a lot to lose in terms of dignity and self-respect and my place in the community. But there's also a lot to gain in terms of finances and I mean, you know, finances that would set me up for life. Take care of me in my old age. Because, well, it's important.

SANDY:
Because when it comes down to it… I guess you just don't want to be alone. You want a friend. And sex is… Well, a way of making a friend. So I thought wow… I've got two freinds now. People I can trust. Because I've tried to trust people. But it's hard. Who you gonna really trust? The guy making the Toyota commercial? The sanitary napkin commercial? The other women all up for the same hooker part, or the topless dancer part… or any other part? No, you can't. It's not possible. You need friends. It's just that kind of life. It's a life when you really need people to be there for you. Listen to you.

SANDY: ...you know, just really be there for you... and...really listen to you.

(The End.)

CRACKPOT

RACHEL WYATT

Rachel Wyatt is one of Canada's best known radio dramatists and has authored over 130 dramas for the CBC and BBC, many of which have gone on to broadcast in other countries. Her works for Canadian radio include *Twenty-One Days*; *Inukshuk*; *Gallery Walk*; *Who Killed Dennis Kline?* and *The Doctor's Casebook*. She has also had three plays produced for stage, *Chairs and Tables* and *Geometry* (both of which premiered at the Tarragon Theatre) and the stage adaptation of *Crackpot*, which premiered at Alberta Theatre Projects in 1995 to wild acclaim. She has written four novels, including *Time in the Air* and *Foreign Bodies*, and, most recently, a collection of short stories, *The Day Marlene Dietrich Died*. Rachel has been involved with the Writing Program at the Banff Centre for the Arts for ten years, and has been its Director for five. She also taught at the Arctic College summer school on Baffin Island for a number of years. Rachel lives in Victoria, British Columbia.

Crackpot was first broadcast on *Stereodrama*, on March 14, 1994
with the following cast:

HODA .... Donna Goodhand

DANILE .... Wes Tritter

POLONICK .... Brian McKay

UNCLE NATE .... James Brewer

LIMPY LETZ .... Christopher Hunt

MORGAN .... Daryl Shuttleworth

MISS FLAKE .... Kate Newby

MISS BOTHOLMSUP .... Jane Logie

GUSIA .... Maureen Thomas

MRS LETZ .... Judith Buchan

YANKL .... Bartley Bard

PIPICK/DAVID .... Stephen Sparks

LAZAR .... Ian D. Clark

Producer .... Martie Fishman

Recording Engineer .... Bob Doble

Sound Effects .... Ute Shaffland

Music .... Amin Bhatia

Executive Producer .... James Roy

Script Editor .... Dave Carley

Prologue

> *(All these voices are remote, tangential. Some more remote than others.)*

HODA: Tell me the story, Daddy.

DANILE: You wouldn't believe our luck. For on the surface, aren't we the unluckiest people on the earth?

VOICES: Hoda! Hoda! Fat pig, Hoda. Crackpot, Hoda!

MOTHER: What were you and your friends playing out in the shed, Hoda?

HODA: Doctors and nurses, Ma.

DANILE: Miracle! Our little girl wants to be a doctor.

HODA: I like being the patient too, Daddy.

MOTHER: God forbid you should be a patient like me... *(Build to scream.)*

HODA: I've never slept with anyone all night before. My son. My son.

DAVID: Mother?

LAZAR: We'll forget the past and live together?

DAVID: She lived her life backwards don't you see.

DANILE: God only *seems* to punish.

DAVID: Lived her life backwards.

MOTHER: *(Quiet agony.)* A patient like me.

> *(Fade on soft scream.)*

Scene One

(It is about 1912, Winnipeg. The outside street sounds are of pedestrians, horse-drawn vehicles— but this isn't a through street. Inside HODA's house, she and DANILE are crying softly.)

HODA: I'll look after you, Daddy.

DANILE: Your mother, Hoda. What a good woman.

HODA: See how all the people came to mourn for her, Daddy.

DANILE: And we never lacked a minyan for the prayers.

HODA: All the food they brought.

DANILE: Good thing your mother made me go to the classes, eh Hoda. So now I can make baskets.

HODA: I'll sell them. I'll put signs up. Wickerwork. Straw chairs.

DANILE: Stop! Baskets only for now.

HODA: We'll have a shop with a window.

DANILE: And an office with books and a clerk.

HODA: And I'll work behind the counter, I'll wear a flowered dress.

DANILE: Your uncle, my mother's brother. He'll come back. He came to sit shiva with us. To mourn for your mother.

HODA: All the time before he never came to visit.

DANILE: He'll look after us. You'll see. Didn't he bring us out here to Canada? Me and your mother, though I wasn't a prize exactly. Maybe not what he was expecting. A nephew who couldn't see. A niece a little misshapen. And you, a baby. But his own flesh and blood. My mother's brother.

(Fade DANILE's voice to:)

Scene Two

(Inside UNCLE NATE's house.)

GUSIA: What am I telling you!

UNCLE: It's my family.

GUSIA: Your *sister's* family, Nate.

UNCLE: What's this, Gusia?

GUSIA: A cake. A cake I made to give them. Then maybe you won't give away our money.

UNCLE: You gave them a cake already.

GUSIA: Take it.

UNCLE: My sister, healthy as two women, almost as big as me. Stays behind in the old country. Has to let herself get dragged off by cholera. And what do I get! The only family I have left so I bring my nephew and his wife to Canada like a brother should for his sister's child. Did she ever tell me her son was blind! Always my sweet Danile this, my dear Danile that, never a word he couldn't see. So what turns up here on my doorstep, ten years ago almost to the day! Three sacks. A lumpy sack, a blind sack and their kid the over-stuffed sack.

GUSIA: Not a penny of our money goes to them. You hear.

UNCLE: Not enough the sack has to embarrass me cleaning people's houses right here in town. Now she has to die.

GUSIA: Not a penny!

UNCLE: Leave me alone.

(Sound: Door slams.)

Scene Three

(Inside HODA's house. Sound: HODA setting out cups on table.)

DANILE: So you see, Hoda, if I hadn't been blind and your
             mother a little crooked in the back, many things
             would never have happened. And you, probably,
             would never have been born.

             (Sound: Loud knock at the door. Door opening.)

UNCLE: Shalom.

HODA: Uncle Nate!

UNCLE: Shalom.

DANILE: Was machts du.

UNCLE: In your time of sorrow.

HODA: Sit down, Uncle.

UNCLE: Where? Where will I sit?

HODA: This is the best chair.

UNCLE: My wife sent you this cake.

DANILE: You're very welcome in my home.

HODA: Tea. I'll make tea. You'd like tea.

UNCLE: Don't fuss. You've grown to be a big girl…a very
             big girl. Ten, eleven, are you?

HODA: Eleven.

DANILE: How's your wife? Your boys?

UNCLE: My wife is—herself. My boys, they're growing.

HODA: My cousins.

UNCLE: So this is how you live?

HODA: Daddy's making mats for the floor. Baskets, mats,
             he makes. I'm going to sell them and…

UNCLE: And what are you going to live on, meanwhile?
             (Beat.) How do you plan to eat!

HODA: Cake, Uncle? Tea?

UNCLE: Stop bothering me. I want to tell you what I've done for you.

DANILE: I knew. My mother's brother. I knew you would come to our rescue.

HODA: Thank you, Uncle.

UNCLE: Get away from me. Let me speak. Yesterday I went to the Jewish Home for the Aged and the Jewish Children's Home and I made a generous donation to each of them.

DANILE: Hear that, Hoda. A generous donation.

UNCLE: The supervisor of the children's home, a good man, friend of mine. Samuel is his name. And you can be there tomorrow, Hoda. I'll come and take you there, myself. You pack up your things like a good girl.

HODA: My things?

UNCLE: And you, Danile, you'll be with others, you'll be cared for...

DANILE: A home!

HODA: (Yelling.) Nooooo! You can't take me away from my Daddy. I'll look after him. I can clean and cook.

UNCLE: (Shouting.) You're a kid. A fat kid. You don't know what's best.

HODA: For who best! I won't leave my Daddy. Never. (Yells.) Never!

UNCLE: I was tricked into bringing you nothings to the New World and now you want to shame me living in this—place—in the same...my wife...

            (HODA snivelling, crying.)

            Tell that kid of yours her nose is running. *Wipe your nose!*

            (HODA cries louder.)

DANILE: (*Quietly.*) It's good your sister, my mother, is dead
               that she can't see how you treat your own family.
               You have contracted the strangers' disease.
               Inhumanity.

HODA: We're not going. We stay together.

DANILE: We will manage.

UNCLE: You'll be sorry. You'll come to me begging yet.

HODA: We won't. We won't. We won't.

               (*Sound: Door slamming. UNCLE crashing down
               the steps, cursing.*)

               He's broken the verandah.

DANILE: It's a good thing his sister, my mother...is dead. A
               good thing your mother's father, the soldier, Shem
               Berl, is not aware.

               (*Music bridge: Old country music—a violin
               playing something plaintive.*)

Scene Four

               (*In the street: Winnipeg 1914.*)

GUSIA: So she's cleaning your house. Two years her
               mother's been dead and she cleans the same
               houses.

MRS. LETZ: That Hoda. Sure. She cleans. She cleans out my
               shelves, my icebox. Eat! I never saw someone eat so
               much.

GUSIA: What'll she do if we get food rationing?

MRS.
PANKESS: She wiggles that fat ass of hers as she does the
               floors. If she was nice-looking, I'd worry my Yankl
               would...

GUSIA: See there she goes into your Yankl's shop now.

MRS. LETZ: And what can she afford to buy? Steak!

(Women laugh. Fade laughter to:)

Scene Five

(In the butcher's shop.)

YANKL: So good-day to you, Mrs. Cohen. Enjoy the chicken.

MRS. COHEN: See you next week, Yankl.

(Sound: Door closing.)

YANKL: You, Hoda. What do you want?

HODA: Something to make soup with, please.

YANKL: (Mocking.) Something to make soup with? You haven't paid for the bones I gave you last week.

HODA: Next week I'll have money. Next week…

YANKL: Next week you'll owe me for two weeks. Week after that for three…

HODA: My daddy needs soup. We—

YANKL: Don't cry, kid. Listen. (Enticing.) Come round this side of the counter, Hoda. C'mon. You're not such a little girl now.

HODA: Yankl. I can't. I don't.

YANKL: You get meat and soup for nothing if you just do this for me.

HODA: It's not right.

YANKL: Is it right you want my stock and you don't pay?

HODA: (Whimpering a little.) No.

YANKL: Lots of nice soup for your Daddy, Hoda.

HODA: I don't know what you want from me.

YANKL: Give me your hand.

(HODA makes a sound of disgust.)

Just…down. There. Right out of sight.

(Sound: Bell shop door.)

(Low.) That's right, Hoda.

(Beat.)

Good morning, Mrs. Letz. What can I do for you?

MRS. LETZ: I thought I saw Hoda come in here.

YANKL: She. Mmm. Well. She…she's maybe out back.

MRS. LETZ: You alright, Yankl?

YANKL: *(Groans a little.)* Fine. Fine.

MRS. LETZ: Then I'll have two pounds of tripe and…

YANKL: Two pounds—of—tripe.

MRS. LETZ: What'll happen to us if this war comes?

YANKL: *(Gasping a little.)* I don't know, Mrs. Letz. I really don't know.

        (Sound: Distant gunfire. Fade guns to music: "Soldiers of the Queen".)

Scene Six

        (In the schoolroom.)

MISS FLAKE: As I was telling you, class, our brave boys are over there fighting to save dear old England and we must all do whatever we can.

HODA: I saw England once, Miss Flake. On the way here. I was only a baby but my daddy said…

MISS FLAKE: That's enough, Hoda. Get on with your knitting.

HODA: And he held me up to show me where the King lives.

MISS FLAKE: Ah, the Royal Family. The Prince of Wales I've seen with my own eyes.

HODA: What does a prince look like?

MISS FLAKE: Very, very royal. And yet when he looks straight at you, you know that in that moment, he's thinking only of you... His eyes just looking into yours... *(Beat.)* What is it, Hoda?

HODA: I can't...

MISS FLAKE: What is this!

HODA: *(Sniffling.)* I don't know knitting.

MISS FLAKE: What soldier is going to want to wear a sock this shape and this colour?

(Class laughs.)

HODA: Things get dirty on their own. It's not my fault.

MISS FLAKE: Don't cry, Hoda. I'll give you one last chance. Now go and pull this out and begin again.

HODA: *(Softly.)* Tell more about the prince.

MISS FLAKE: Several times I waited outside the palace in London and he always, always came out and waved. If I waited long enough.

(Music: "Soldiers of the Queen".)

(Under.) So remember there's a war on. Now get to work.

(Music up to:)

Scene Seven

(At home.)

DANILE: If I weren't a blind man, Hodaleh, I could be fighting, like Shem Berl.

HODA: And what would I do then, Daddy?

                 (Sound: Knock at the door.)

POLONICK: It's me, Polonick.

DANILE: Come in. Come in, Mr. Polonick.

HODA: Soup? There's enough if you'd like some.

DANILE: Yankl, the butcher, is very generous to us.

POLONICK: Thank you. Thank you. No. I've come to see why
                 you aren't coming to Yiddish School Hoda.

HODA: Sssh. Some days.

DANILE: Not going to Yiddish school? But every afternoon,
                 she goes.

HODA: Some days I go. Other days…

POLONICK: Other days, cleaning, playing with friends… But no
                 reproaches today.

DANILE: It's a holiday?

POLONICK: We're beginning to look to Russia, Danile. The
                 workers here have to understand. Tyrants can be
                 overthrown.

HODA: Tea. I'll make some tea.

POLONICK: In Russia, the oppressed are rising. And I'll tell you
                 something else, it won't be long before that
                 happens here too. When the soldiers come back.
                 And people are starving, low wages, lousy
                 conditions. And all the employers say is if you
                 don't like it, leave. So leave! You'll see. And you,
                 how do you manage?

DANILE: Hoda sells my baskets.

POLONICK: There will be revolution.

                 (Music: "The Internationale".)

Scene Eight

> (*At home. Next morning.*)

DANILE: My father, though he was only a tailor by trade, was a wise man.

HODA: I've got to get to school, Daddy.

DANILE: That's right, study, study.

HODA: Today it's my turn to make a presentation. We have to tell something about our lives the teacher says. So I'm telling about you and Momma.

DANILE: (*Fading.*) It was a hot clammy day when they carried me from the house. I struggled like a wild thing, slithering about in their hands and my sweat. They tried to explain to me what they were going to do but all I knew was it was wrong to leave my sick mother.

> (*Music: Dark wedding music to:*)

Scene Nine

> (*At school. A restless class.*)

HODA: My father has been blind most of his life and my mother, well, she had one shoulder higher than the other so she looked a little hunchbacked.

> (*Class murmurs.*)

MISS
BOTHOLMSUP: Now then, class. Let's hear what Hoda has to say.

HODA: Thank you, Miss Bottomsup.

MISS
BOTHOLMSUP: BotTOMsup, Hoda.

HODA: (*Nervous, trying to get it right.*) Yes Miss BottomSUP.

MISS
BOTHOLMSUP: Continue.

HODA: How I came to be born. It was the time of the plague
                 where my parents were in the old country.
                 Everybody was dying. Especially all the Christians
                 were dying. And they knew that the Jews could
                 stop the plague if they wanted. And they came to
                 them and begged them.

                     (Class murmurs.)

                 There's only one way to stop the plague. You have
                 to get two people to kind of marry each other in the
                 graveyard. Two poor people. And they knew they
                 had to do this and thank goodness for me they did
                 or I might not be here. So they took my Daddy,
                 crying and screaming, and my Momma to where
                 the canopy was and after the ceremony, they laid
                 them down on top of the graves and…

                     (Class murmurs excitedly.)

MISS
BOTHOLMSUP: Hoda!

HODA: And then they had to, while people were
                 watching…

MISS
BOTHOLMSUP: Hoda!!!

HODA: So they…

MISS
BOTHOLMSUP: We've heard enough, Hoda.

HODA: *(Distressed.)* I haven't finished. I haven't said what
                 happened. How I came to be born and…

MISS
BOTHOLMSUP: Go and sit down.

HODA: You said if we told about ourselves, we'd get to
                 understand each other and—

MISS
BOTHOLMSUP: Enough.

HODA: Sorry Miss Bottomsup.

MISS
BOTHOLMSUP: BotTOMSup.

HODA: Sorry Miss BOTTOMSUP.

(Class titters.)

MISS
BOTHOLMSUP: That's all for today, class. Now we'll all sing our national anthem and as you march out, think about this great country we live in.

(Class singing "The Maple Leaf Forever". Footsteps. Class leaving.)

Come here Hoda. I know you did your best, Hoda, but there are things that are not suitable. Not just what you said…but look at you.

(HODA sniffs.)

You know as well as I do your tunic should be regulation length, six inches above the ankle. What is one to think of a girl who wears her tunic almost as short as her knickers? I ask you.

HODA: I haven't got any money.

MISS
BOTHOLMSUP: Never mind. Just pay attention to what I've said.

HODA: But you should've let me say…

MISS
BOTHOLMSUP: Dismissed.

Scene Ten

(The street: Light car traffic, slow. On the way home.)

MORGAN: I liked what you were telling, Hoda.

HODA: Did you, Morgan? *(Sniffs.)* I'd worked real hard on it and I hadn't got to the real part where…

MORGAN:	What does she know, old assendup? So did the plague go away?
HODA:	Not only went away. Some people even got better. So they knew it had worked.
MORGAN:	Your dad was sort of a hero.
HODA:	And my mom too. Yes.
LIMPY:	Hey, Morg! Leave the fat kid alone and come and shoot craps.
MORGAN:	I'll win all your money, Limpy.
LIMPY:	Whyn't we play for Hoda?
HODA:	Oh sure! Get lost Limpy Letz.
LIMPY:	We know what you do for Yankl the butcher.
MORGAN:	Leave her alone.
LIMPY:	Tell you what, Hoda. Winner gets you. You get the pot. Might be a couple of dollars.
HODA:	*(Hesitant.)* OK, but only if it's Morgan.

(Fade sounds of boys shooting dice.)

Scene Eleven

(The school basement. HODA and MORGAN making love.)

HODA: You got to say I love you when you do it, Morgan.

(MORGAN grunts.)

Say it. Say I love you.

MORGAN: *(With effort.)* I love you I love you I love you.

("I love you" reverbs with different voices if possible.)

HODA: I love you too, Morgan.

(Both sigh. Sound of scuffling as they re-arrange their clothes.)

MORGAN: But hey, Hoda. The other guys got money, you know. You put out for them. They'll pay.

(Bridge to: HODA walking home. Traffic sounds in background.)

Scene Twelve

HODA: He said I love you. He didn't mean it. I could tell. He only said it 'cause I told him to. *(Beat.)* We could sure use the money. But I did it. Did I really do it? Is that what it's all about? Will they know? Will people be able to tell? Can they see from my face? *(Beat.)* It felt good. Felt really good. And Miss Bottomsup what would she say? Who cares about her anyway. I bet nobody ever shot craps for her.

MRS.
POLONICK: Hello, Hoda.

HODA: *(Absent-mindedly.)* Hello, Mrs. Polonick.

(Walking on.)

And nobody can tell me what to do. I'll fuck them all if I like. Daddy wouldn't like it. Momma wouldn't like it. Well, what did she have to go and die for. Other kids' mothers hardly ever die. I'm sorry Momma. I won't do it again. Ever. They can beg and beg and I won't ever do it again.

(Sound: Footsteps fading. Music: Old country to "The Maple Leaf Forever".)

Scene Thirteen

(HODA's house. HODA counting money into DANILE's hand.)

HODA: See Daddy. One dollar. A quarter. Two dimes…

DANILE: You shouldn't stay out so late selling baskets, little girl.

HODA: They're good baskets.

DANILE: I counted. There seem to be as many left as there were before…

HODA: Tell me about Shem Berl, Daddy. I'll heat up the soup. Tell me about the Russian war.

DANILE: Him and his pots and pans. He was a tinker. They made him fight in the Czar's army. A simple, trusting soul. When his first five years were up, they put a paper in front of him…and can he read Russian? No! So he's signed on for another five years.

HODA: And what about now, Daddy? Now the Czar is gone.

DANILE: Who knows, Hoda. Not that he didn't deserve it, the Czar, but what will become of the old country now.

HODA: And maybe grandfather is free?

                 (Sound: Knock at door.)

POLONICK: It's me, Polonick.

DANILE: Come in, Mr. Polonick. Come in. Sit down. You've come to tell me how well Hoda's doing at Yiddish school.

POLONICK: Who can think of Yiddish school when the Czar…the Czar, Danile, has at last been overthrown by the people.

DANILE: The Czar. I heard. Whose side will the Russians fight on now?

POLONICK: Their own, comrade. And about time too. They're free! Free.

DANILE: Hear that, Hoda. A people can get free.

HODA: And my grandfather, Shem Berl?

POLONICK: Fighting for the Red Army, I've no doubt.

HODA: Boys I knew at school are going off to fight.

(Music: Military band under:)

DANILE: When your grandfather had served all his time in the Cossack Army he got home at last to find all the women crying. They were about to take his son into the army. So what did he do, Shem Berl, hero that he was, he turned right around and went off to serve the boy's time too.

(Music to:)

Scene Fourteen

(At the house.)

DANILE: It was a terrible time, Hoda. The time of the plague. So many dying. Soon there wasn't a clove of garlic left in the whole city.

HODA: I like about the garlic.

(Sound: Knock at door. Voices of HODA's friends outside.)

DANILE: Who's that?

HODA: Some of my friends come to read with me, Daddy. C'mon on in, Limpy. Morgan.

DANILE: Study. That's good. My father though only a tailor by trade—

HODA: We'll go to my room.

DANILE: That's right. So you have peace.

(Boys laugh.)

LIMPY: *(Low.)* My turn, Hoda.

HODA: Come on then.

Scene Fifteen

(HODA's room. DANILE can be heard in the other room singing Yiddish syllables to "Oh God our help in ages past". Sound of scuffling.)

LIMPY: Hoda. Hoda-a-a-a.

HODA: You'll have to be quiet, Limpy, so my Daddy doesn't hear.

LIMPY: I can't be quiet. Whew! Hoda.

HODA: You're a nice guy, Limpy. But you're noisy.

LIMPY: So why don't you clear a place in that shed out back…

HODA: OK. But for now you owe me seventy-five cents.

LIMPY: Fifty!

HODA: You got to take one of Daddy's baskets.

LIMPY: I don't want a basket.

HODA: You gotta buy a basket or no you-know-what.

LIMPY: Alright. Alright. Give me a basket. But not every time.

               (Limpy exits. DANILE is still singing. HODA calls out to DANILE.)

HODA: I didn't know you knew that song, Daddy. The choir used to sing it at school. In the mornings.

DANILE: I learnt it at the Centre, at basket-making school. It's a song of the blind.

HODA: Your baskets are selling real well, Daddy.

               (Fade DANILE singing to:)

Scene Sixteen

(In the street.)

MRS. LETZ: That Hoda, she came to my Ruthie's wedding. Ate all the food and danced as if she'd been invited.

GUSIA: They say you can't have a wedding now but there she is. It's unlucky if she's not there.

MRS. POLONICK: She cleans for me. I told her, you're a fat pig, Hoda. You should quit eating a while.

MRS. LETZ: And how they manage. My husband bought me one of her father's baskets.

GUSIA: So did mine. You should help the blind. It's a mitzvah.

MRS. POLONICK: And my Jerry bought me one too.

(A moment of silence.)

ALL TOGETHER: Hoda!!!

Scene Seventeen

(1925. At home.)

DANILE: Who would've thought that I, a blind man, would ever get to see the New World. And not only that, would live like a prince.

HODA: The Prince is coming Daddy. Here to Winnipeg. The Prince of Wales.

DANILE: He and the Czar were related. Cousins maybe.

HODA: He's not married. He's looking for the right woman. I just know it. And how to find her with all those overdressed stuck-up people he has to go around with.

DANILE: They tell me he and the Czar look like twins.

HODA: One thing about being big like me, Daddy, you
               stand out in a crowd. So maybe the Prince will
               notice me. It said in the paper he danced with this
               one and that one at the ball and is a man of the
               people. Not just the Prince of Wales.

               (Dream music: Gypsy violins.)

               (Voice over:) And he will realise that I am everything
               he needs in a Queen. And I'll sweep up the aisle
               with that crown on my head and not care how
               heavy it is. And I'll be loving to him always. I'll
               learn how to curtsey. And people will curtsey to me
               as I walk by.

DANILE: My daughter, to marry a gentile. An Englishman.
               But a prince!

HODA: And at first Queen Mary will be surprised but then
               she'll understand. We're in love, Your Majesty, we
               shall say. Your son has realised that all he ever
               wanted was a big girl, like me. I'll be like Queen
               Esther, Daddy. I'll save the country from war and
               plague too. My prince, my Prince of Wales.

               (Dreamy wedding music to:)

Scene Eighteen

               (Sound: Loud knocking at the door. Door opening.)

POLONICK: Hey, it's me, Polonick. C'mon Hoda. It's time for
               the demonstration.

HODA: And the Prince of Wales…

DANILE: So the prince is coming here, to Winnipeg.

HODA: You can demonstrate, Mr. Polonick. I have to stand
               where the prince can see me.

POLONICK: You want to look at royalty, Hoda, when the
               workers are shouting for their rights.

HODA: How often does the Prince come this way.

DANILE: I should come too.

POLONICK: It's a dangerous crowd, Danile. You're safer here.

HODA: I'll tell you all about it, Daddy.

DANILE: Take care of my little girl, Polonick.

               (Sound: Door.)

Scene Nineteen

               (Walking along the street. At the beginning the sound of the crowd is very distant but comes closer as they approach it.)

POLONICK: When the revolution comes here the first thing I'm going to do is liberate you, Hoda. We'll put the fun and freedom back in fucking.

HODA: What will I do for a living, comrade? How will I feed my daddy?

POLONICK: You'll get an honest job, Hoda. Your days will be spent in building the public paradise and your nights will be spent in building the private paradise.

HODA: Comes the revolution, maybe your old lady won't have to work so hard. You'll stay home in your own private paradise.

POLONICK: With my wife! For this I manned the barricades!

               (Sounds of crowd as they get nearer. Shouts of workers:)

WORKER 1:   A living wage.

WORKER 2:   A twelve hour day.

WORKER 3:   Give us freedom.

WORKER 1:   The cops.

HODA:	Let me through. Let me through. The Prince needs to see me. I have to get to the front.
	(The women are off to one side but the crowd and shouting can still be heard.)
MRS. LETZ:	See that Hoda. Always shoving.
MRS. POLONICK:	The war over nearly ten years and still no one's happy.
GUSIA:	Those strikers. On such a day. When royalty's here. They could shoot them for all I care.
MRS. LETZ:	That's treason.
MRS. POLONICK:	The strikers she's talking about!
GUSIA:	See the police. Stand back.
MRS. LETZ:	What will the Prince think?
MRS. POLONICK:	How often does a prince come to Winnipeg?
MRS. LETZ:	You can say you're not interested but a man who'll be king is a somebody.
GUSIA:	The police'll get them off the street before he comes by.
	(Sounds of strikers rises.)
VOICES:	Treat us like slaves. "Shut up and starve." Not only in Russia, eh. That's what they're telling us, "Shut up and starve." Who fought in the war!
COP:	Get back. Get back.
	(Fighting. Uproar.)
POLONICK:	Workers of the world… Aaargh…
HODA:	Mr. Polonick!
COP:	Back.

HODA: Get back you. Dumb cop. Leave that man alone…

          (Sound as she grabs the cop and pulls him off his horse. Cop falling off horse.)

COP: Yaargh!

HODA: Come on, Mr. Polonick.

          (Sound: Running footsteps. Heavy breathing. Riot sound receding to the distance. HODA and POLONICK are out of breath.)

          The Prince never got to see me.

POLONICK: Who needs Royalty!

HODA: I do. I have. I wanted him.

POLONICK: You fought like a cossack, Hoda.

HODA: He never saw me.

POLONICK: Like a cossack.

HODA: My grandfather Shem Berl fought for the cossacks.

POLONICK: Others talk. They see the truncheon bearing down. They're afraid. I was afraid. But you. You hit back.

HODA: I wasn't going to let that dumb cop conk you on the head.

POLONICK: Come on. Before they come back.

HODA: I can't run any more.

POLONICK: You stay in the house a few days. You don't want to end up in jail.

HODA: Jail! It would drive Uncle mad. Worth it maybe. My niece the jailbird.

POLONICK: And listen, Hoda. I'd like for you to come to one of our meetings…

HODA: I'd be honoured, Mr. Polonick.

          (The "The Internationale".)

POLONICK: Our newest member. Some of you know her pretty well already. Like her grandfather, she's a hero. She fought that policeman like a bulldog.

HODA: Honoured Mr. Polonick.

POLONICK: Let's all welcome Hoda.

("Hoda" echoes and very loud cheers fade to:)

HODA: Honoured, Mr. Polonick.

Scene Twenty

(At home.)

DANILE: You're not feeling well, Hoda. Here's milk for you.

HODA: Must've twisted something when I pulled that cop off his horse.

DANILE: Mr. Polonick says you're a hero. Your mother should've lived to see this. So you do take after your grandfather.

HODA: *(Through pain.)* Shem Berl.

DANILE: But you should be more careful.

HODA: It hurts a little, that's all.

DANILE: Stay in bed, Hodaleh. I can manage.

HODA: This pain in my insides. It keeps coming back.

DANILE: *(Smiling.)* It's going around. Remember your mother's joke.

Something that's going around.

HODA: *(To herself.)* Going around. Turning somersaults. Something huge turning somersaults inside me.

DANILE: Drink your milk, Hodaleh. And sleep—sleep. *(Echo.)* Sleep well.

(Bridge to HODA's room at night.)

Scene Twenty-One

(HODA's room at night. In HODA's mind: All the
voices remote:)

HODA: Who are you? Who're all of you?

DAVID: Living your life backwards, mother.

DANILE: And there in the graveyard…

MISS
BOTHOLMSUP: What becomes of a girl who wears her tunic as short
as her knickers.

BOYS: We can see your ass, Hoda.

YANKL: Do this for me, Hoda. I'll give you all the soup
bones you want.

POLONICK: I am the Prince of Wales. I've come to ask for your
hand…

HODA: No you're not. You're Polonick.

(Sound of building crashing down.)

GUSIA: The orphanage is collapsing.

UNCLE: All my money falling down.

MORGAN: I love you, Hoda. Love you.

(Several saying "I love you" dying away as orgasm.)

DANILE: So when we got to the New World…

(Music: Crashing chord. End of unreality.)

HODA: Please Daddy, please Mommy, please God, help
me. (Moans.) Aaargh. (Softly.) Help me somebody.
I'm dying. I'm dead. (Groans. Moans.) It's a dream.
Something in the bed. Ooooh. No. Daddy. Mamma.
Mamma. I'm dying. I'm dead… Mustn't wake
Daddy. Mustn't wake… Aaaargh…

(Sound of shuffling, HODA moaning, the baby
being born. Baby squawks.)

What are you? Who are you? Baby. A baby. My
baby. Shhh. *(Beat.)* This cord. It's gotta be cut, baby.
I'm going to bite it. Ready! Ach! Quiet. I didn't
know. I didn't know. Why're your little eyes glued
together? It's got to be a dream. *(Beat.)* You're really
there aren't you? A nose. A mouth. Two legs. A tiny
whatnot. Oh baby! Daddy mustn't know about this.
What am I to do with you? Hide you? Give you
away? Please God help me. An orphan. A little
orphan.

(Baby sounds.)

Stay there while I clean up this mess. Get this
mattress outside.

*(Sound: Mattress being moved with effort.
Outside.)*

It's an ordinary fine night with stars and all and it's
quiet and I'm standing here with a mattress soaked
in blood and inside there, inside. It isn't true. When
I go back it will all be gone. And this is a dream.
Even the stars are in on it.

(Sound: HODA returning inside slowly.)

Still here.

(Baby squawks.)

I can't be your mother baby, not really. I don't know
anything about you. And who your father is could
be ten different ones. And me standing there
watching the Prince of Wales. You can't stay here.
You know that. Now then. I gotta write a note for
you. What to say? It all happened so fast because I
went to look for the prince. And who knows who
might be a prince in disguise. *(As she writes.)* Take
good care. A prince in disguise can make a piece of
prince, to save the Jews. He's paid for. Uncle paid
for you, baby. In advance. "I made a generous
donation" he said in that important voice of his. I'll
set you down outside the orphanage, ring the
doorbell.

(Sound: Bell echoing to end of scene.)

And you'll be well looked after. And when I make more money, I'll send that too.

Scene Twenty-Two

(At home. Next morning.)

DANILE: Are you feeling better, Hodaleh?

HODA: Just a little tired. I'll stay in bed today. And maybe tomorrow.

DANILE: You do that. And you'll see what your clever Daddy can fix for you.

HODA: Tell me the story.

DANILE: Well… So when they came for me that day, finally I knew I had to go. I couldn't refuse. And as they led me over the newly dug graves, for one moment I too was brave. I knew what the stars knew. I saw what they saw. And since that moment I have never truly been afraid.

(HODA crying.)

Don't cry, Hodaleh. Don't you see, it worked out alright.

(Up crying and then fade to:)

Scene Twenty-Three

(Women in the street.)

GUSIA: A new baby in the orphanage. Left on the doorstep. A prince!

MRS. LETZ: It's easy for a prince. He says to a lackey, I want this one, I want that one. I want a beautiful Jewish girl.

MRS.
POLONICK: What do we know about royalty!

MRS. LETZ: The swine.

MRS.
POLONICK: She should be ashamed, whoever she is. Her
                forebears would have thrown themselves into the
                fire rather than let him have his way.

GUSIA: Perhaps it was meant we should have a prince.
                Here in our orphanage. My husband's on the
                board, you know.

MRS. LETZ: And we all know what your niece is!

MRS.
POLONICK: That Hoda!

                (They begin to whisper.)

GUSIA: There goes her father to the synagogue.

MRS. LETZ: Mrs. Pankess. See. Going to their place.

MRS.
POLONICK: In a hurry too. Let's go see what she's up to.

                (Sound: Footsteps as they follow MRS. PANKESS.)

MRS.
PANKESS: Where is she! Come out you whore! You husband-
                eater. A present he had to bring me. One of the
                baskets her daddy made. I'll give her present.
                Come out you Delilah.

                (Sound: Door opening.)

HODA: *(Bellowing.)* What do you want?

GUSIA: *(Shrieks.)* She's got no clothes on.

MRS. LETZ: Hoda's got no clothes on.

MRS.
PANKESS: I'll make such a scandal, she'll have to get out of
                town.

HODA: Get away from here.

MRS.
PANKESS: I'll tell that old blind fool your father such a story

his fingers will curl up and he'll never be able to weave again.

HODA: *(Aggressive roar.)* You'll tell my daddy, will you.

MRS.
PANKESS: See. She has the nerve to face me. Naked. Shameless cow.

HODA: Get away from here.

(She begins to chase MRS. PANKESS.)

MRS.
PANKESS: I'll tell the world, you fat cow.

HODA: Who're you calling cow. Call me names, I'll break your neck. Nobody calls me names.

MRS.
PANKESS: You hear her. She wants to kill me. You're all my witness.

(Others laugh.)

(Breathless.) She sleeps with all your husbands.

(Murmur from crowd.)

HODA: See. I still can run. Faster than you. I'll kill you. I will.

MRS.
PANKESS: Whore. Cow! Leave me alone.

(Crowd laughing.)

HODA: *(Short of breath.)* And tell your husband any time he has half a buck.

Scene Twenty-Four

(At home.)

HODA: More tea, Mr. Polonick?

POLONICK: You and your father, Hoda. You're the victims of capitalist brutalization and greed. You have this rich uncle who doesn't think twice about abandoning you to poverty and starvation.

HODA: Uncle is a rat.

DANILE: He has his own family to think of.

POLONICK: You're still stuck with your old-fashioned values, Danile. A man like your uncle...

HODA: Yesterday, I took one of Daddy's baskets to uncle's house and left it on the doorstep with a note. Left him a gift.

POLONICK: Generous Hoda. A bomb you should have left for him. A bomb in a basket. He's rich and he doesn't help his own.

HODA: We manage. Daddy and me.

DANILE: She's a good manager, my Hoda.

POLONICK: Danile! Danile!

DANILE: And one of these days, she'll marry a fine fellow...

(Wedding dance music begins softly and comes up under next scene.)

Scene Twenty-Five

(In the street.)

GUSIA: She goes to every wedding.

MRS. LETZ: Eats the best food.

MRS. POLONICK: Comes to my daughter's wedding. No invitation. So they ask her which side and she says, bold as brass, "Both sides, I'm a friend."

GUSIA: Now they look for her. It's not a proper wedding without Hoda. She brings luck.

MRS. LETZ: Luck! She eats like a vacuum cleaner and they say what she does with the ushers outside...

MRS.
POLONICK: Once even the groom!

            (Fade music.)

Scene Twenty-Six

            *(1934. HODA is 32 or so. At home. There is some
            automobile traffic outside. HODA and the boys,
            now men, are playing cards.)*

LIMPY: That's my queen, Morgan.

MORGAN: That's the fifth queen you've had, Limpy.

LIMPY: Are we playing for Hoda?

MORGAN: We don't have to, do we Hoda?

HODA: Sssh. My Daddy'll hear.

LIMPY: A kiss, Hoda. On account.

HODA: Nothing for nothing.

LIMPY: C'mon.

            *(Sound of horseplay. SFX: Loud knock at the door.
            Door opening.)*

UNCLE: The door needs fixing. Twenty and more years
            since I was here and you haven't fixed the step.

HODA: Uncle Nate! This is a surprise. Out you guys. Come
            back later, OK.

            (Boys exit muttering.)

            I said later!

UNCLE: Tell them I won't stay long.

DANILE: Is that you, Nate?

UNCLE: Sure.

DANILE: *(Weeping.)* Come in. Sit down. Hoda. Tea!

HODA:	Stay for supper, Uncle. I'm fixing offal.
UNCLE:	Like in the old country? I can smell it.
DANILE:	Just like in the old country.
HODA:	Sit down, Uncle.
DANILE:	How are your sons?
UNCLE:	Sons you ask? My sons! To get them to speak to me, I have to buy them a golf course. You've read in the papers. My picture. Me. One of the organizing members of the Jewish Golf Course. You've seen the picture. Well, no, I guess you haven't.
DANILE:	You're an important man now, Nate.
UNCLE:	I can't stay long, but… And for my sins I get to be on the board of the orphanage.
HODA:	The orphanage, Uncle?
UNCLE:	I'm not going to send you there now, Hoda. You're much too big. A good size. A young woman. So I'm at the orphanage and there's old Samuel the superintendant and this new kid, well he's not so new now, the boy, that was left with the note, I am a prince. Prince. Schmince! So he's really attached to old Mrs. Samuel… You're spilling that tea, girl.
HODA:	She's kind to him?
UNCLE:	Follows him round, makes sure he has the best of everything. So she goes to the dorm at night like a scarecrow she is.

(UNCLE gets up and walks around doing actions to his story. HODA laughs softly at first then louder.)

So she has this problem, that she shakes some. And she's thin as a rail. So there she is, her shape in the moonlight bending over the little prince's bed. Tucking him in. The other kids are asleep, having nightmares already and they wake up and see this apparition. Frightens them half to death. So they begin to scream and yell. She looks like a giant spider, you see. Yow. Yow. Yow. So there they all are, hollering, and Samuel comes in and there's pandemonium.

(*Laughs.*)

HODA: (*Close to tears.*) You kill me, Uncle. You should've been a comedian. Gone on the stage.

UNCLE: You know, I thought about it. Years ago. But mouths to feed all around me. Um, um. Ya, ya. Gimme, gimme. Had to make money.

HODA: So he's fine. The little prince?

UNCLE: Fine. They're all fine. Lead lives of Reilly, you ask me.

HODA: Enough to eat?

UNCLE: Plain but plenty. (*Beat.*) One funny thing about that kid, the one that was left on the doorstep. His navel, belly-button it sticks out and it's all twisted.

HODA: (*Faintly.*) How do you know that?

UNCLE: The other boys tease him about it. They call him Pipick. Samuel told me.

HODA: Oh.

(*Sound: Cup dropping and smashing.*)

UNCLE: There now.

HODA: I couldn't help it. Couldn't help it.

(*Fade down and up into UNCLE's second visit.*)

Scene Twenty-Seven

UNCLE: I was telling you, Danile, last time I was here. Samuel I thought was my friend. All I've done for that man. And now as if I was an enemy he treats me.

DANILE: My father, though he was only a tailor by trade, said…

UNCLE:	Since his wife died…
DANILE:	A man in his grief turns bitter. Eats his own entrails.
UNCLE:	Yes. Yes so I'm telling you. And that little guy, the one they call the prince, mopes after she dies. Won't eat, won't sleep.
HODA:	*(From the kitchen.)* What happened to him?
UNCLE:	He's fine now. Kids have short memories. Mine sure do.

(Fade down to later visit. 1938. At home. Sound of marching feet outside, fading.)

UNCLE:	So I'm telling you, Danile, about the orphanage.
DANILE:	I can't believe another war in my lifetime.
UNCLE:	It'll never happen. Chamberlain's gone to Munich.
HODA:	And if it does?
UNCLE:	We'll beat them like last time.
DANILE:	Another war.
UNCLE:	The orphanage, Danile. So now they find that Samuel all that time was interfering with the kids. He's up on charges. And when I think what I did for him. Couldn't keep his hands to himself.
HODA:	The boys!
UNCLE:	Isn't it enough the little girls? So I'm telling you, Danile. Now he's after me, Nate this, Nate will you do that for me.
DANILE:	If there's war, will your sons have to go?
UNCLE:	They're too old, Danile. You forget how the time goes. My sons. I wish. I wish… But there'll be no war. This Hitler's full of wind and water.

(Sound of armies marching to sentimental wartime music like Vera Lynn or "Over there, over there". Long music bridge to:)

Scene Twenty-Eight

(1939. At home.)

DANILE: I wouldn't've believed another war, Hoda. In my lifetime.

HODA: And maybe Shem Berl is still fighting.

DANILE: Who would he be fighting for now? The Russians have signed a pact with the Germans.

HODA: And besides he'd be a hundred and twenty.

DANILE: That means nothing to the generals.

HODA: Uncle's been ill, Daddy.

DANILE: At the synagogue they were talking. His boys are going to put him in the home.

HODA: Poor Uncle.

DANILE: If he'd had a good daughter, like you.

HODA: Daddy!

DANILE: When I was so nervous in the city of the dead, your mother took my hand and helped me with the ring. And when we got back to the house and she saw that my mother was sick, she began to look after her right away. You're just the same, Hoda. An angel.

HODA: Not an angel, Daddy.

DANILE: Argue anything with me. But on that, no argument. You're an angel, my Hodaleh.

HODA: The town is full of soldiers. From the old country, some of them.

(Music:"Over There". HODA under music.)

Come to Momma Hoda. An army marches on its stomach. And here's the stomach you should march on. Have some fun before you go. Over there...over there. You'll be back when it's over, over there.

(Fade music to:)

Scene Twenty-Nine

(HODA's room.)

PIPICK: Hello.

HODA: Hello. This your first time?

PIPICK: No. I done it lots of times.

HODA: Close the door. Relax. You got to learn to take it easy.

PIPICK: I know. I know.

HODA: It's your money. You want to get the most out of it. Guys have said to me, I never knew what it could be like till I did it with you, solo. The lousy way of life we got here, it cripples people. I got some customers don't even know any better. Whang whang, in and out. They've been stunted from childhood. Sometimes I think what's going to happen when I get up there and the Almighty says, "Alright, Hoda, what've you been doing all these years." And I'll say, "Well, Lord, I made a little love." And he'll say, "Not bad, Hoda. I ain't done much more myself."

(She laughs. He laughs.)

So why don't you take your clothes off. What's your name, kid? Not your whole name, just something to call you by.

PIPICK: David. My clothes?

HODA: Sure. You work better without them. Don't be shy. Believe me, I've seen everything. What're you keeping covered up there? Come here then.

(A few sighs and moans.)

Hey. What's this? What's wrong, kid. I hurt you?

PIPICK: I'm not a kid. It's my navel, that's all. It's weird. It makes me feel like a freak.

HODA: Ssshhh. You'll wake my father.

PIPICK: I don't care about your father.

HODA: Let's forget it then. I don't care about your pipick. I think it's kind of cute. Look, we're wasting your time over nothing.

PIPICK: It's not nothing. All my life they've teased me about it. Prince Pipick.

HODA: Prince?

PIPICK: I don't care if my father was a prince.

HODA: *(First glimmer of recognition.)* So your dad's a prince?

PIPICK: I wish they'd left me out on the step to freeze.

HODA: What step? What freeze?

PIPICK: I wish my belly button had burst open and let me die. I didn't ask to be alive.

HODA: Come on. Don't talk like that. You're making all this up.

PIPICK: I am not.

HODA: *(Stunned.)* You shouldn't tell lies like that. It's alright by me, your father's a grocer, a peddler. Maybe you should go home to your ma and pa till you feel better.

PIPICK: I'm not a goddamn liar. I haven't got any goddamn ma and pa. I'm a goddamn bastard prince! And I can prove it. I can prove it!

HODA: Prove! Who cares what you can prove!

PIPICK: Nobody calls me a liar!

(He gets some papers out of his pants pocket.)

HODA: What is this? What is it?

PIPICK: These envelopes. See. For the Prince. This note. *He's paid for!*

HODA: You stole those.

PIPICK: *(Shouting.)* You calling me a thief and a liar.

HODA: *(Whispers.)* I'm sorry. I just lost my temper. I thought you were trying to pull a fast one.

PIPICK: So come on, Hoda. Come back here.

HODA: I'm just feeling a little strange.

PIPICK: I thought you liked me. We were making love you said. Not like the other guys.

HODA: No. I mean yes. But why should a nice clean kid like you come to someone like me. I know class when I see it. I'm too old for you—David. And I'm…I'm…

PIPICK: It's alright. I'm not a snob. How could I be. Growing up there.

HODA: You had a rotten time. All this time? I'm sorry.

PIPICK: There was a kind woman. But she died. Look, let's not talk about all that. I want…I want.

HODA: Wait a minute.

PIPICK: So let me. Let me. Let me…

HODA: *(A very difficult decision.)* Come here then.

(Music to:)

Scene Thirty

(At home.)

DANILE: So did I ever tell you, Hoda—

HODA: You told me. You told me. You told me. Over and
           over. I don't want to hear your stories any more,
           Daddy.

           (HODA crying.)

DANILE: *(Tentative.)* We yearn for the Leviathan but in our
           hunger we worship the humble schmaltz herring.

HODA: What are you talking about, Pa?

DANILE: You and the Prince of Wales…it made me think.

           (Both laugh. She through tears.)

HODA: It's too late. I should've written him a long time ago
           and told him he was making a mistake. So he had to
           go and marry a commoner anyway and give up the
           throne. And over there, they call them kippers,
           Daddy.

DANILE: So don't cry, my Hodaleh.

HODA: It's not that prince I'm crying for. *(To herself.)* My
           boy. My boy grown. How can I tell him. He knows
           what I am. I can give myself a grand title, 'Sexual
           Worker, Reasonable Rates'. Give up my profession
           then get married. What a joke. Who'd have me? I'm
           an old maid practically. And if anybody turned up
           who wanted me, what kind of a guy would he be, to
           want everybody's warmed-over leftovers! And if I
           got married and then said to the guy, see, I happen
           to have this grown-up son. *(Beat.)* No stepfather's
           going to mistreat my boy. Let him try! I want to go
           backwards, back to the night he was born, keep him
           myself, me and Daddy. Daddy, this is your
           grandson… And what would the boy say to me, his
           mother. Everybody knows what I am… There's no
           way, no way, no way.

DANILE: By the time I was seven years old, Hodaleh, seven
           only, I was already going blind. Why did you have
           to stare at the sun, my mother said… Only fools and
           children stare at the sun.

HODA: Shut up, Daddy. Blind! Blind! Is that all you think
           about.

(Sound: Door slamming. Bridge to:)

Scene Thirty-One

(Women in the street.)

GUSIA: You've seen that Hoda.

MRS. LETZ: Goes to every funeral.

MRS.
POLONICK: Wears black. Weeps.

GUSIA: You can't help wondering.

MRS. LETZ: Where does all that weeping come from.

MRS.
POLONICK: A past like hers.

GUSIA: And with the war, you'd think she could find something better to do.

(Fade street sounds to:)

Scene Thirty-Two

(At home.)

HODA: How're you doing, David?

DAVID: I'll be doing better in a few minutes.

HODA: Not today.

DAVID: I can pay.

(He brings out a roll of bills.)

HODA: Where d'you get all that money?

DAVID: It's mine. Sent to me, Old Poppov's been keeping it for me in a drawer in his office.

HODA: Does he know you've got it?

DAVID: He shouldn't have shown it to me.

HODA: So you took it.

DAVID: I took it for you. For you.

HODA: But I meant it…

DAVID: For you.

HODA: Listen to me, David. You're a nice boy. I'd rather be your friend. I want you to save your money for schoolbooks. You want to save yourself too. I know guys, they started too young. By the time they're thirty-five, not a bang left in them.

DAVID: Don't worry about me. I'll have plenty left.

HODA: It's not good for you. You'll go from bad to worse and end up your whole life wasted like me.

DAVID: Your life's not wasted. You're the best thing that's ever happened to me.

HODA: Oh David. Oh David. So sit by me. Talk.

DAVID: (Shouting.) I don't want to talk.

HODA: (Yelling back.) Well, talk's all you're going to get from me.

        (Cut to:)

Scene Thirty-Three

        (Women in the street.)

GUSIA: They say the young prince…

MRS. LETZ: Young thief.

MRS.
POLONICK: Ran off with all the money from the orphanage.

GUSIA: I never believed he was a prince.

MRS. LETZ: They said it was money sent for him by his father, the prince, and kept in a drawer for him.

GUSIA:	A fortune in gold.
MRS. LETZ:	He's lied about his age and joined the army.
GUSIA:	The war'll be over soon, they say.
MRS. LETZ:	They've been saying that for years.
MRS. POLONICK:	I've knitted socks till my fingers are near worn through.
GUSIA:	Isn't that Hoda going into your son's delicatessen, Mrs. Letz?
MRS. LETZ:	He's been a friend of hers…just a good friend, mind you, since school.
MRS. POLONICK:	Just a good friend!
GUSIA:	She's kept pretty busy, all these foreign soldiers in town. Poles, Belgians, French.
MRS. LETZ:	And the guy from Galicia they say was in the camps and got away.
GUSIA:	In the camps.

(Soft music to:)

Scene Thirty-Four

(Customers. Counter sounds.)

LIMPY:	Corned beef on rye for thirteen. Chicken soup. Latkes. No latkes like mine anywhere.
HODA:	You're doing well, Limpy. You always said when you were a kid, you'd own a restaurant.
LIMPY:	I want to tell you, Hoda.
HODA:	I know. I know. I'll leave if you like.
LIMPY:	I don't mind if you come here every day.
HODA:	This place needs a good scrub, Limpy.

LIMPY: You could help other ways, Hoda. Help with the cash. Sometimes the tables. It's a better line of work for you.

HODA: Get me off my back eh, Limpy?

                (She laughs. Echo the laugh.)

LIMPY: And bring your Dad. There's a warm corner for him.

                (Sound of people in the deli, chatting, laughing.)

DANILE: *(Part of his story.)* And so you see we came to this country, to Canada. And when the officials come I'm holding the book and the baby, just like my wife told me. And she's whispering to me, "Wrong way up. Wrong way up." And I think she means the baby and I turn her the other way up. Poor little thing she enters her new home upside down.

LAZAR: It's a fine story.

                (Fade deli sounds.)

Scene Thirty-Five

                (At home.)

DANILE: Why are you crying, my Hodaleh?

HODA: Mr. Polonick, Daddy. His funeral.

DANILE: What would he have said to you?

HODA: Weep for the living. But I want to weep for him, Daddy. He was a friend when we didn't have many friends.

DANILE: You have a good heart, Hoda. And I wish. I wish…

                (Cut to:)

Scene Thirty-Six

       (The deli.)

LIMPY: I want to make you a proposition, Hoda.

HODA: You don't have to, Limpy. You're one of my oldest customers. You and Morgan.

LIMPY: I'm offering you a job. Here at the deli.

HODA: You're going to pay me to be here, talk to my friends?

LIMPY: You attract people, Hoda. They enjoy themselves when you're around.

HODA: There's truth in that.

LIMPY: My wife said…well, never mind what she said. I told her if she thought she could bring the guys in like you do, she's welcome to try.

       (HODA laughs.)

       And that guy from Galicia, that Lazar, has his eye on you. So watch out.

HODA: He walks me home, that's all.

       (Deli sound and music up then down to:)

Scene Thirty-Seven

       (The street, a cold night. Sound: Footsteps on snow.)

HODA: OK, so I'm not the Duchess of Windsor. Once I thought the Prince… Once I thought… But who'd be in their shoes, royalty. They've got their troubles. I got mine.

LAZAR: Two can live…

HODA: I need to get married like I need a hole in the head. Wait up a minute.

LAZAR: Let me carry that for you, Hoda.

HODA: I can manage. My own burdens I've always carried.

LAZAR: We could be happy together maybe.

HODA: I mean it. Happiness I don't know. But comfort I got. My Daddy is alright. He coughs some but... *(To herself.)* Happiness? It's a word. We've managed. Is that happiness? We love each other, my daddy and me. Is that happiness? He lives in ignorance, my dad. Is that happiness?

(Sound of footseps on the snow only for a moment.)

LAZAR: *(Something in garbled Yiddish.)*

HODA: How do you expect me to understand what you're saying in Galician? You call that Yiddish. I'd understand you better in Chinese, or Scandihoovian.

LAZAR: Not much I can say.

HODA: What do you need me for. I mean you know what I am. I'm not ashamed of what I am. I don't want anybody telling afterwards how they took me off the streets and made a mensch of me. And you. Haven't you had enough trouble in your life? Out there, in the camps?

LAZAR: I keep coming to the deli for you, Hoda.

HODA: So it's my fault. It's my fault you come there every night and throw your money away on cards.

LAZAR: I can't just come there and sit, Hoda. It's a business like any other. Limpy's got to make a living. I come there and sit, he's going to say, "What's this, a deepee schnorrer I don't need, taking up a chair where a customer could be laying eggs."

HODA: If I want a friend of mine to come and sit, he comes and sits. And it's not for Limpy to tell you where to lay your eggs either.

LAZAR: I'll lay my eggs wherever you like, Hoda.

(HODA laughs.)

If I'm not there, you walk home with whoever loses at cards because you feel sorry for him.

HODA: So!

LAZAR: I don't want anybody walking you home but me, Hoda.

(Footsteps taper to:)

Scene Thirty-Eight

(At home.)

HODA: The Galitzianer wants to marry me, Daddy.

DANILE: When. Have you decided when?

HODA: What do you mean when! You don't even know who? *(Beat.)* You've been talking.

DANILE: He's a fine man, Lazar. An educated man. A man it's a pleasure to talk to. And what that man has suffered.

HODA: How come you know about his suffering. Why didn't you tell me you talked to him?

DANILE: *(Gently.)* I didn't want to interfere, Hoda. It's none of my business.

HODA: Who said you'd be interfering! It's your business if I get married. Since when am I so hard to talk to. Since when am I so hard to get along with!

DANILE: If you were hard to get along with would I lie to him? Would I spend hours telling him the opposite. What a sunny-natured little girl you were. How you were the smile in my heart, the sight in my eyes. How you used to trudge around to sell the baskets. Didn't I know it was bitter for you! And all those boys. The English words they use. You staying up so late. And I'd hear you crying. So you stayed up a little late. What right had I to interfere. I know how hard things were in those days for you. I explained to him.

HODA: Explained. Daddy. You knew…

DANILE: A blind man can't shut his eyes to what he knows.

(A fragment of silence.)

HODA: You want me to get married, Daddy? Or is it just his story you like?

DANILE: Who could like such a story. The cruellest thing about being blind is you can't close your eyes to what you see. He was plucked alive from that dead flesh, dragged himself away…

HODA: You want me to marry him?

DANILE: I wasn't such a bargain either when they brought me to your mother.

HODA: Oh Papa.

(HODA laughs. He joins in.)

DANILE: And she put her little hand on mine, helped me with the ring…

(Cut to:)

Scene Thirty-Nine

(At the deli. Music.)

HODA: Hey Limpy! Did the Galitzianer come in tonight?

LIMPY: Haven't seen him in two nights.

HODA: Anyone seen the Galitzianer?

CUSTOMER: You gone monogamous lately, Hoda?

(HODA laughs. Sound: Teapot smashed.)

HODA: See. Look what you made me do. I'll get you another teapot, Limpy.

LIMPY: Go home, Hoda. It's late.

HODA: I've got to clean up. Wipe the counters.

LIMPY: Cheaper if I do it myself tonight. Go home.

                (Fade deli sounds to:)

Scene Forty

                (On the street. Footsteps crunching on snow.)

HODA: *(To herself.)* So who needs the Galitzianer. I'm not
                surprised. Not a bit surprised. Proposals are easy.
                He got frightened, the deepee schnorrer.
                Frightened I'd say yes. He's run away. Made me a
                laughing stock. Asks me to marry him. Then runs
                away.

                (Walking in the snow.)

LAZAR: You're late, Hoda.

HODA: *(Yelling.)* You. You mocky. What do you think
                you're doing. No don't explain. I don't want to
                hear. Just go away. You're a… Go screw yourself.
                Mocky. Mocky. Mocky! *(Sniffs.)*

LAZAR: You're crying.

HODA: I'm sorry I called you names.

LAZAR: So what is it, Mocky? In my language it's Maw-kee.
                Plague. Curse. The cursed one. You're right to send
                the cursed one away.

HODA: It's not Maw-kee. It's mocky, mocky. A name. A
                joke.

                (Footsteps only.)

                Why have you been talking about me to my father
                behind my back?

LAZAR: Because it's time you give up the life you lead and
                settle down.

HODA: Is that so? A new life. Who're you to be handing out new lives. Why should I forget the past. It's all I've got. All that's my own. All that's here, inside me, that is mine.

               (She cries.)

LAZAR: Should I have died then? *(Beat.)* Should I not have dragged myself out from under the bodies? Flesh of my father, flesh of my sister, flesh of my whole world, I gripped them and crawled over them...

               (He cries.)

               Help me, Hodaleh. I don't ask you to share it. Just be with me.

HODA: *(Through tears.)* I'll help you. Honest I will. Two broken down old crocks like us, Lazar. What are we doing wandering round the street late at night. I'm sorry I called you names but when you didn't turn up at Limpy's Deli tonight, I couldn't stand it. *(Beat.)* Listen, if I'm engaged, where's my ring?

LAZAR: You'll have your ring.

HODA: I've changed my mind. I don't want a ring. We'll put a payment on a house and have a bedroom set first. All white furniture with a gold effect.

               (Music: Discordant romantic.)

Scene Forty-One

               (HODA and LAZAR in bed. LAZAR snores a little.)

HODA: We'll get a wall-to-wall mattress.

LAZAR: *(In sleep.)* I'm glad I found you, Hodaleh. You're squashing me, Hoda.

HODA: I'm sorry. I've never slept...spent the whole night with anyone before.

(LAZAR snores lightly again. Dream music. Hints of violins, Royal wedding, marching band. In dream from now to end.)

I've got to remember this when I wake up.

(Sound: Wreckers knocking down a building.)

That's the orphanage. They're tearing it down. Here little Danny. Stand by me. Something I have to tell you. *Cherish your corpses. They give your life body.*

GUSIA: Crackpot Hoda. Have respect.

POLONICK: A heroine, Hoda.

DAVID: *(In wonder.)* You lived your life backwards, mother.

HODA: See now, I curtsey to you all. To you, Prince, to you Duchess, to you poor Uncle, to you and you...

(Music up to end.)

LAZAR: Sleep gently, Hoda.

DANILE: My father, though only a tailor by trade, was a wise man...

(The End.)

All inquiries concerning performing rights, readings or any other use of:

The Mercy Quilt should be directed to
    The Playwrights Union of Canada
    54 Wolseley Street, 2nd Floor
    Toronto, Ontario, Canada M5T 1A5
    Tel: (416) 703-0201

Mourning Dove should be directed to
    The Playwrights Union of Canada
    54 Wolseley Street, 2nd Floor
    Toronto, Ontario, Canada M5T 1A5
    Tel: (416) 703-0201

Stop Talking Like That should be directed to
    Great North Artists Management Inc.
    350 Dupont Street
    Toronto, Ontario, Canada M5R 1V9
    Tel: (416) 925-2051

How to Make Love to an Actor should be directed to
    Great North Artists Management Inc.
    350 Dupont Street
    Toronto, Ontario, Canada M5R 1V9
    Tel: (416) 925-2051

Crackpot should be directed to
    Patricia Ney, Christopher Banks and Associates
    6 Adelaide Street East, Suite 610
    Toronto, Ontario, Canada M5C 1H6
    Tel: (416) 214-1155